FREE Study Skills DVD Offer

Dear Customer,

Thank you for your purchase from Mometrix! We consider it an honor and a privilege that you have purchased our product and we want to ensure your satisfaction.

As a way of showing our appreciation and to help us better serve you, we have developed a Study Skills DVD that we would like to give you for <u>FREE</u>. This DVD covers our *best practices* for getting ready for your exam, from how to use our study materials to how to best prepare for the day of the test.

All that we ask is that you email us with feedback that would describe your experience so far with our product. Good, bad, or indifferent, we want to know what you think!

To get your FREE Study Skills DVD, email <u>freedvd@mometrix.com</u> with *FREE STUDY SKILLS DVD* in the subject line and the following information in the body of the email:

- The name of the product you purchased.
- Your product rating on a scale of 1-5, with 5 being the highest rating.
- Your feedback. It can be long, short, or anything in between. We just want to know your impressions and experience so far with our product. (Good feedback might include how our study material met your needs and ways we might be able to make it even better. You could highlight features that you found helpful or features that you think we should add.)
- Your full name and shipping address where you would like us to send your free DVD.

If you have any questions or concerns, please don't hesitate to contact me directly.

Thanks again!

Sincerely,

Jay Willis
Vice President
<u>jay.willis@mometrix.com</u>
1-800-673-8175

GRE

Prep 2020 & 2021

GRE Secrets Study Book

Full-Length Practice Test

Detailed Answer Explanations

Includes Step-by-Step Review Video Tutorials

Written and edited by the Mometrix Graduate School Admissions Test Team

Printed in the United States of America

This paper meets the requirements of ANSI/NISO Z39.48-1992 (Permanence of Paper).

Mometrix offers volume discount pricing to institutions. For more information or a price quote, please contact our sales department at sales@mometrix.com or 888-248-1219.

Paperback
ISBN 13: 978-1-5167-1242-7
ISBN 10: 1-5167-1242-0

DEAR FUTURE EXAM SUCCESS STORY

First of all, **THANK YOU** for purchasing Mometrix study materials!

Second, congratulations! You are one of the few determined test-takers who are committed to doing whatever it takes to excel on your exam. **You have come to the right place.** We developed these study materials with one goal in mind: to deliver you the information you need in a format that's concise and easy to use.

In addition to optimizing your guide for the content of the test, we've outlined our recommended steps for breaking down the preparation process into small, attainable goals so you can make sure you stay on track.

We've also analyzed the entire test-taking process, identifying the most common pitfalls and showing how you can overcome them and be ready for any curveball the test throws you.

Standardized testing is one of the biggest obstacles on your road to success, which only increases the importance of doing well in the high-pressure, high-stakes environment of test day. Your results on this test could have a significant impact on your future, and this guide provides the information and practical advice to help you achieve your full potential on test day.

Your success is our success

We would love to hear from you! If you would like to share the story of your exam success or if you have any questions or comments in regard to our products, please contact us at **800-673-8175** or **support@mometrix.com**.

Thanks again for your business and we wish you continued success!

Sincerely,
The Mometrix Test Preparation Team

Need more help? Check out our flashcards at:
http://mometrixflashcards.com/GRE

TABLE OF CONTENTS

INTRODUCTION 1

SECRET KEY #1 – PLAN BIG, STUDY SMALL 2

SECRET KEY #2 – MAKE YOUR STUDYING COUNT 3

SECRET KEY #3 – PRACTICE THE RIGHT WAY 4

SECRET KEY #4 – PACE YOURSELF 6

SECRET KEY #5 – HAVE A PLAN FOR GUESSING 7

TEST-TAKING STRATEGIES 10

VERBAL REASONING TEST 15
    SENTENCE EQUIVALENCE 15
    TEXT COMPLETION 18
    READING COMPREHENSION 21
    FINAL WARNINGS 27

QUANTITATIVE REASONING TEST 28
    QUANTITATIVE COMPARISON 29
    NUMBERS AND OPERATIONS 30
    DATA ANALYSIS, PROBABILITY, AND STATISTICS 44
    MEASUREMENT AND GEOMETRY 48

ANALYTICAL WRITING TEST 59
    ISSUE ANALYSIS 60
    ARGUMENT ANALYSIS 64
    FINAL NOTE 69

GRE PRACTICE TEST 70
    SECTION 1 70
    ANALYTICAL WRITING 70
    SECTION 2 71
    ANALYTICAL WRITING 71
    SECTION 3 72
    VERBAL REASONING 72
    SECTION 4 80
    VERBAL REASONING 80
    SECTION 5 87
    QUANTITATIVE REASONING 87
    SECTION 6 95
    QUANTITATIVE REASONING 95

ANSWER KEY 102

ANSWER EXPLANATIONS 103
    SECTION 3 103
    VERBAL REASONING 103
    SECTION 4 108

VERBAL REASONING _____108
SECTION 5_____114
QUANTITATIVE REASONING_____114
SECTION 6_____117
QUANTITATIVE REASONING_____117

HOW TO OVERCOME TEST ANXIETY _____ **120**
CAUSES OF TEST ANXIETY _____120
ELEMENTS OF TEST ANXIETY _____121
EFFECTS OF TEST ANXIETY_____121
PHYSICAL STEPS FOR BEATING TEST ANXIETY _____122
MENTAL STEPS FOR BEATING TEST ANXIETY_____123
STUDY STRATEGY_____124
TEST TIPS _____126
IMPORTANT QUALIFICATION _____127

HOW TO OVERCOME YOUR FEAR OF MATH _____ **128**
FALSE BELIEFS _____129
MATH STRATEGIES_____131
TEACHING TIPS _____133
SELF-CHECK _____134

THANK YOU _____ **135**

ADDITIONAL BONUS MATERIAL _____ **136**

Introduction

Thank you for purchasing this resource! You have made the choice to prepare yourself for a test that could have a huge impact on your future, and this guide is designed to help you be fully ready for test day. Obviously, it's important to have a solid understanding of the test material, but you also need to be prepared for the unique environment and stressors of the test, so that you can perform to the best of your abilities.

For this purpose, the first section that appears in this guide is the **Secret Keys**. We've devoted countless hours to meticulously researching what works and what doesn't, and we've boiled down our findings to the five most impactful steps you can take to improve your performance on the test. We start at the beginning with study planning and move through the preparation process, all the way to the testing strategies that will help you get the most out of what you know when you're finally sitting in front of the test.

We recommend that you start preparing for your test as far in advance as possible. However, if you've bought this guide as a last-minute study resource and only have a few days before your test, we recommend that you skip over the first two Secret Keys since they address a long-term study plan.

If you struggle with **test anxiety**, we strongly encourage you to check out our recommendations for how you can overcome it. Test anxiety is a formidable foe, but it can be beaten, and we want to make sure you have the tools you need to defeat it.

Secret Key #1 – Plan Big, Study Small

There's a lot riding on your performance. If you want to ace this test, you're going to need to keep your skills sharp and the material fresh in your mind. You need a plan that lets you review everything you need to know while still fitting in your schedule. We'll break this strategy down into three categories.

Information Organization

Start with the information you already have: the official test outline. From this, you can make a complete list of all the concepts you need to cover before the test. Organize these concepts into groups that can be studied together, and create a list of any related vocabulary you need to learn so you can brush up on any difficult terms. You'll want to keep this vocabulary list handy once you actually start studying since you may need to add to it along the way.

Time Management

Once you have your set of study concepts, decide how to spread them out over the time you have left before the test. Break your study plan into small, clear goals so you have a manageable task for each day and know exactly what you're doing. Then just focus on one small step at a time. When you manage your time this way, you don't need to spend hours at a time studying. Studying a small block of content for a short period each day helps you retain information better and avoid stressing over how much you have left to do. You can relax knowing that you have a plan to cover everything in time. In order for this strategy to be effective though, you have to start studying early and stick to your schedule. Avoid the exhaustion and futility that comes from last-minute cramming!

Study Environment

The environment you study in has a big impact on your learning. Studying in a coffee shop, while probably more enjoyable, is not likely to be as fruitful as studying in a quiet room. It's important to keep distractions to a minimum. You're only planning to study for a short block of time, so make the most of it. Don't pause to check your phone or get up to find a snack. It's also important to **avoid multitasking**. Research has consistently shown that multitasking will make your studying dramatically less effective. Your study area should also be comfortable and well-lit so you don't have the distraction of straining your eyes or sitting on an uncomfortable chair.

The time of day you study is also important. You want to be rested and alert. Don't wait until just before bedtime. Study when you'll be most likely to comprehend and remember. Even better, if you know what time of day your test will be, set that time aside for study. That way your brain will be used to working on that subject at that specific time and you'll have a better chance of recalling information.

Finally, it can be helpful to team up with others who are studying for the same test. Your actual studying should be done in as isolated an environment as possible, but the work of organizing the information and setting up the study plan can be divided up. In between study sessions, you can discuss with your teammates the concepts that you're all studying and quiz each other on the details. Just be sure that your teammates are as serious about the test as you are. If you find that your study time is being replaced with social time, you might need to find a new team.

Secret Key #2 – Make Your Studying Count

You're devoting a lot of time and effort to preparing for this test, so you want to be absolutely certain it will pay off. This means doing more than just reading the content and hoping you can remember it on test day. It's important to make every minute of study count. There are two main areas you can focus on to make your studying count:

Retention

It doesn't matter how much time you study if you can't remember the material. You need to make sure you are retaining the concepts. To check your retention of the information you're learning, try recalling it at later times with minimal prompting. Try carrying around flashcards and glance at one or two from time to time or ask a friend who's also studying for the test to quiz you.

To enhance your retention, look for ways to put the information into practice so that you can apply it rather than simply recalling it. If you're using the information in practical ways, it will be much easier to remember. Similarly, it helps to solidify a concept in your mind if you're not only reading it to yourself but also explaining it to someone else. Ask a friend to let you teach them about a concept you're a little shaky on (or speak aloud to an imaginary audience if necessary). As you try to summarize, define, give examples, and answer your friend's questions, you'll understand the concepts better and they will stay with you longer. Finally, step back for a big picture view and ask yourself how each piece of information fits with the whole subject. When you link the different concepts together and see them working together as a whole, it's easier to remember the individual components.

Finally, practice showing your work on any multi-step problems, even if you're just studying. Writing out each step you take to solve a problem will help solidify the process in your mind, and you'll be more likely to remember it during the test.

Modality

Modality simply refers to the means or method by which you study. Choosing a study modality that fits your own individual learning style is crucial. No two people learn best in exactly the same way, so it's important to know your strengths and use them to your advantage.

For example, if you learn best by visualization, focus on visualizing a concept in your mind and draw an image or a diagram. Try color-coding your notes, illustrating them, or creating symbols that will trigger your mind to recall a learned concept. If you learn best by hearing or discussing information, find a study partner who learns the same way or read aloud to yourself. Think about how to put the information in your own words. Imagine that you are giving a lecture on the topic and record yourself so you can listen to it later.

For any learning style, flashcards can be helpful. Organize the information so you can take advantage of spare moments to review. Underline key words or phrases. Use different colors for different categories. Mnemonic devices (such as creating a short list in which every item starts with the same letter) can also help with retention. Find what works best for you and use it to store the information in your mind most effectively and easily.

Secret Key #3 – Practice the Right Way

Your success on test day depends not only on how many hours you put into preparing, but also on whether you prepared the right way. It's good to check along the way to see if your studying is paying off. One of the most effective ways to do this is by taking practice tests to evaluate your progress. Practice tests are useful because they show exactly where you need to improve. Every time you take a practice test, pay special attention to these three groups of questions:

- The questions you got wrong
- The questions you had to guess on, even if you guessed right
- The questions you found difficult or slow to work through

This will show you exactly what your weak areas are, and where you need to devote more study time. Ask yourself why each of these questions gave you trouble. Was it because you didn't understand the material? Was it because you didn't remember the vocabulary? Do you need more repetitions on this type of question to build speed and confidence? Dig into those questions and figure out how you can strengthen your weak areas as you go back to review the material.

Additionally, many practice tests have a section explaining the answer choices. It can be tempting to read the explanation and think that you now have a good understanding of the concept. However, an explanation likely only covers part of the question's broader context. Even if the explanation makes sense, **go back and investigate** every concept related to the question until you're positive you have a thorough understanding.

As you go along, keep in mind that the practice test is just that: practice. Memorizing these questions and answers will not be very helpful on the actual test because it is unlikely to have any of the same exact questions. If you only know the right answers to the sample questions, you won't be prepared for the real thing. **Study the concepts** until you understand them fully, and then you'll be able to answer any question that shows up on the test.

It's important to wait on the practice tests until you're ready. If you take a test on your first day of study, you may be overwhelmed by the amount of material covered and how much you need to learn. Work up to it gradually.

On test day, you'll need to be prepared for answering questions, managing your time, and using the test-taking strategies you've learned. It's a lot to balance, like a mental marathon that will have a big impact on your future. Like training for a marathon, you'll need to start slowly and work your way up. When test day arrives, you'll be ready.

Start with the strategies you've read in the first two Secret Keys—plan your course and study in the way that works best for you. If you have time, consider using multiple study resources to get different approaches to the same concepts. It can be helpful to see difficult concepts from more than one angle. Then find a good source for practice tests. Many times, the test website will suggest potential study resources or provide sample tests.

Practice Test Strategy

If you're able to find at least three practice tests, we recommend this strategy:

UNTIMED AND OPEN-BOOK PRACTICE

Take the first test with no time constraints and with your notes and study guide handy. Take your time and focus on applying the strategies you've learned.

TIMED AND OPEN-BOOK PRACTICE

Take the second practice test open-book as well, but set a timer and practice pacing yourself to finish in time.

TIMED AND CLOSED-BOOK PRACTICE

Take any other practice tests as if it were test day. Set a timer and put away your study materials. Sit at a table or desk in a quiet room, imagine yourself at the testing center, and answer questions as quickly and accurately as possible.

Keep repeating timed and closed-book tests on a regular basis until you run out of practice tests or it's time for the actual test. Your mind will be ready for the schedule and stress of test day, and you'll be able to focus on recalling the material you've learned.

Secret Key #4 – Pace Yourself

Once you're fully prepared for the material on the test, your biggest challenge on test day will be managing your time. Just knowing that the clock is ticking can make you panic even if you have plenty of time left. Work on pacing yourself so you can build confidence against the time constraints of the exam. Pacing is a difficult skill to master, especially in a high-pressure environment, so **practice is vital**.

Set time expectations for your pace based on how much time is available. For example, if a section has 60 questions and the time limit is 30 minutes, you know you have to average 30 seconds or less per question in order to answer them all. Although 30 seconds is the hard limit, set 25 seconds per question as your goal, so you reserve extra time to spend on harder questions. When you budget extra time for the harder questions, you no longer have any reason to stress when those questions take longer to answer.

Don't let this time expectation distract you from working through the test at a calm, steady pace, but keep it in mind so you don't spend too much time on any one question. Recognize that taking extra time on one question you don't understand may keep you from answering two that you do understand later in the test. If your time limit for a question is up and you're still not sure of the answer, mark it and move on, and come back to it later if the time and the test format allow. If the testing format doesn't allow you to return to earlier questions, just make an educated guess; then put it out of your mind and move on.

On the easier questions, be careful not to rush. It may seem wise to hurry through them so you have more time for the challenging ones, but it's not worth missing one if you know the concept and just didn't take the time to read the question fully. Work efficiently but make sure you understand the question and have looked at all of the answer choices, since more than one may seem right at first.

Even if you're paying attention to the time, you may find yourself a little behind at some point. You should speed up to get back on track, but do so wisely. Don't panic; just take a few seconds less on each question until you're caught up. Don't guess without thinking, but do look through the answer choices and eliminate any you know are wrong. If you can get down to two choices, it is often worthwhile to guess from those. Once you've chosen an answer, move on and don't dwell on any that you skipped or had to hurry through. If a question was taking too long, chances are it was one of the harder ones, so you weren't as likely to get it right anyway.

On the other hand, if you find yourself getting ahead of schedule, it may be beneficial to slow down a little. The more quickly you work, the more likely you are to make a careless mistake that will affect your score. You've budgeted time for each question, so don't be afraid to spend that time. Practice an efficient but careful pace to get the most out of the time you have.

Secret Key #5 – Have a Plan for Guessing

When you're taking the test, you may find yourself stuck on a question. Some of the answer choices seem better than others, but you don't see the one answer choice that is obviously correct. What do you do?

The scenario described above is very common, yet most test takers have not effectively prepared for it. Developing and practicing a plan for guessing may be one of the single most effective uses of your time as you get ready for the exam.

In developing your plan for guessing, there are three questions to address:

- When should you start the guessing process?
- How should you narrow down the choices?
- Which answer should you choose?

When to Start the Guessing Process

Unless your plan for guessing is to select C every time (which, despite its merits, is not what we recommend), you need to leave yourself enough time to apply your answer elimination strategies. Since you have a limited amount of time for each question, that means that if you're going to give yourself the best shot at guessing correctly, you have to decide quickly whether or not you will guess.

Of course, the best-case scenario is that you don't have to guess at all, so first, see if you can answer the question based on your knowledge of the subject and basic reasoning skills. Focus on the key words in the question and try to jog your memory of related topics. Give yourself a chance to bring the knowledge to mind, but once you realize that you don't have (or you can't access) the knowledge you need to answer the question, it's time to start the guessing process.

It's almost always better to start the guessing process too early than too late. It only takes a few seconds to remember something and answer the question from knowledge. Carefully eliminating wrong answer choices takes longer. Plus, going through the process of eliminating answer choices can actually help jog your memory.

Summary: Start the guessing process as soon as you decide that you can't answer the question based on your knowledge.

How to Narrow Down the Choices

The next chapter in this book (**Test-Taking Strategies**) includes a wide range of strategies for how to approach questions and how to look for answer choices to eliminate. You will definitely want to read those carefully, practice them, and figure out which ones work best for you. Here though, we're going to address a mindset rather than a particular strategy.

Your chances of guessing an answer correctly depend on how many options you are choosing from.

How many choices you have	How likely you are to guess correctly
5	20%
4	25%
3	33%
2	50%
1	100%

You can see from this chart just how valuable it is to be able to eliminate incorrect answers and make an educated guess, but there are two things that many test takers do that cause them to miss out on the benefits of guessing:

- Accidentally eliminating the correct answer
- Selecting an answer based on an impression

We'll look at the first one here, and the second one in the next section.

To avoid accidentally eliminating the correct answer, we recommend a thought exercise called **the $5 challenge**. In this challenge, you only eliminate an answer choice from contention if you are willing to bet $5 on it being wrong. Why $5? Five dollars is a small but not insignificant amount of money. It's an amount you could afford to lose but wouldn't want to throw away. And while losing $5 once might not hurt too much, doing it twenty times will set you back $100. In the same way, each small decision you make—eliminating a choice here, guessing on a question there—won't by itself impact your score very much, but when you put them all together, they can make a big difference. By holding each answer choice elimination decision to a higher standard, you can reduce the risk of accidentally eliminating the correct answer.

The $5 challenge can also be applied in a positive sense: If you are willing to bet $5 that an answer choice *is* correct, go ahead and mark it as correct.

Summary: Only eliminate an answer choice if you are willing to bet $5 that it is wrong.

Which Answer to Choose

You're taking the test. You've run into a hard question and decided you'll have to guess. You've eliminated all the answer choices you're willing to bet $5 on. Now you have to pick an answer. Why do we even need to talk about this? Why can't you just pick whichever one you feel like when the time comes?

The answer to these questions is that if you don't come into the test with a plan, you'll rely on your impression to select an answer choice, and if you do that, you risk falling into a trap. The test writers know that everyone who takes their test will be guessing on some of the questions, so they intentionally write wrong answer choices to seem plausible. You still have to pick an answer though, and if the wrong answer choices are designed to look right, how can you ever be sure that you're not falling for their trap? The best solution we've found to this dilemma is to take the decision out of your hands entirely. Here is the process we recommend:

Once you've eliminated any choices that you are confident (willing to bet $5) are wrong, select the first remaining choice as your answer.

Whether you choose to select the first remaining choice, the second, or the last, the important thing is that you use some preselected standard. Using this approach guarantees that you will not be enticed into selecting an answer choice that looks right, because you are not basing your decision on how the answer choices look.

This is not meant to make you question your knowledge. Instead, it is to help you recognize the difference between your knowledge and your impressions. There's a huge difference between thinking an answer is right because of what you know, and thinking an answer is right because it looks or sounds like it should be right.

Summary: To ensure that your selection is appropriately random, make a predetermined selection from among all answer choices you have not eliminated.

Test-Taking Strategies

This section contains a list of test-taking strategies that you may find helpful as you work through the test. By taking what you know and applying logical thought, you can maximize your chances of answering any question correctly!

It is very important to realize that every question is different and every person is different: no single strategy will work on every question, and no single strategy will work for every person. That's why we've included all of them here, so you can try them out and determine which ones work best for different types of questions and which ones work best for you.

Question Strategies

READ CAREFULLY

Read the question and answer choices carefully. Don't miss the question because you misread the terms. You have plenty of time to read each question thoroughly and make sure you understand what is being asked. Yet a happy medium must be attained, so don't waste too much time. You must read carefully, but efficiently.

CONTEXTUAL CLUES

Look for contextual clues. If the question includes a word you are not familiar with, look at the immediate context for some indication of what the word might mean. Contextual clues can often give you all the information you need to decipher the meaning of an unfamiliar word. Even if you can't determine the meaning, you may be able to narrow down the possibilities enough to make a solid guess at the answer to the question.

PREFIXES

If you're having trouble with a word in the question or answer choices, try dissecting it. Take advantage of every clue that the word might include. Prefixes and suffixes can be a huge help. Usually they allow you to determine a basic meaning. Pre- means before, post- means after, pro - is positive, de- is negative. From prefixes and suffixes, you can get an idea of the general meaning of the word and try to put it into context.

HEDGE WORDS

Watch out for critical hedge words, such as *likely, may, can, sometimes, often, almost, mostly, usually, generally, rarely,* and *sometimes*. Question writers insert these hedge phrases to cover every possibility. Often an answer choice will be wrong simply because it leaves no room for exception. Be on guard for answer choices that have definitive words such as *exactly* and *always*.

SWITCHBACK WORDS

Stay alert for *switchbacks*. These are the words and phrases frequently used to alert you to shifts in thought. The most common switchback words are *but, although*, and *however*. Others include *nevertheless, on the other hand, even though, while, in spite of, despite, regardless of*. Switchback words are important to catch because they can change the direction of the question or an answer choice.

10

FACE VALUE

When in doubt, use common sense. Accept the situation in the problem at face value. Don't read too much into it. These problems will not require you to make wild assumptions. If you have to go beyond creativity and warp time or space in order to have an answer choice fit the question, then you should move on and consider the other answer choices. These are normal problems rooted in reality. The applicable relationship or explanation may not be readily apparent, but it is there for you to figure out. Use your common sense to interpret anything that isn't clear.

Answer Choice Strategies

ANSWER SELECTION

The most thorough way to pick an answer choice is to identify and eliminate wrong answers until only one is left, then confirm it is the correct answer. Sometimes an answer choice may immediately seem right, but be careful. The test writers will usually put more than one reasonable answer choice on each question, so take a second to read all of them and make sure that the other choices are not equally obvious. As long as you have time left, it is better to read every answer choice than to pick the first one that looks right without checking the others.

ANSWER CHOICE FAMILIES

An answer choice family consists of two (in rare cases, three) answer choices that are very similar in construction and cannot all be true at the same time. If you see two answer choices that are direct opposites or parallels, one of them is usually the correct answer. For instance, if one answer choice says that quantity x increases and another either says that quantity x decreases (opposite) or says that quantity y increases (parallel), then those answer choices would fall into the same family. An answer choice that doesn't match the construction of the answer choice family is more likely to be incorrect. Most questions will not have answer choice families, but when they do appear, you should be prepared to recognize them.

ELIMINATE ANSWERS

Eliminate answer choices as soon as you realize they are wrong, but make sure you consider all possibilities. If you are eliminating answer choices and realize that the last one you are left with is also wrong, don't panic. Start over and consider each choice again. There may be something you missed the first time that you will realize on the second pass.

AVOID FACT TRAPS

Don't be distracted by an answer choice that is factually true but doesn't answer the question. You are looking for the choice that answers the question. Stay focused on what the question is asking for so you don't accidentally pick an answer that is true but incorrect. Always go back to the question and make sure the answer choice you've selected actually answers the question and is not merely a true statement.

EXTREME STATEMENTS

In general, you should avoid answers that put forth extreme actions as standard practice or proclaim controversial ideas as established fact. An answer choice that states the "process should be used in certain situations, if..." is much more likely to be correct than one that states the "process should be discontinued completely." The first is a calm rational statement and doesn't even make a definitive, uncompromising stance, using a hedge word *if* to provide wiggle room, whereas the second choice is a radical idea and far more extreme.

BENCHMARK

As you read through the answer choices and you come across one that seems to answer the question well, mentally select that answer choice. This is not your final answer, but it's the one that will help you evaluate the other answer choices. The one that you selected is your benchmark or standard for judging each of the other answer choices. Every other answer choice must be compared to your benchmark. That choice is correct until proven otherwise by another answer choice beating it. If you find a better answer, then that one becomes your new benchmark. Once you've decided that no other choice answers the question as well as your benchmark, you have your final answer.

PREDICT THE ANSWER

Before you even start looking at the answer choices, it is often best to try to predict the answer. When you come up with the answer on your own, it is easier to avoid distractions and traps because you will know exactly what to look for. The right answer choice is unlikely to be word-for-word what you came up with, but it should be a close match. Even if you are confident that you have the right answer, you should still take the time to read each option before moving on.

General Strategies

TOUGH QUESTIONS

If you are stumped on a problem or it appears too hard or too difficult, don't waste time. Move on! Remember though, if you can quickly check for obviously incorrect answer choices, your chances of guessing correctly are greatly improved. Before you completely give up, at least try to knock out a couple of possible answers. Eliminate what you can and then guess at the remaining answer choices before moving on.

CHECK YOUR WORK

Since you will probably not know every term listed and the answer to every question, it is important that you get credit for the ones that you do know. Don't miss any questions through careless mistakes. If at all possible, try to take a second to look back over your answer selection and make sure you've selected the correct answer choice and haven't made a costly careless mistake (such as marking an answer choice that you didn't mean to mark). This quick double check should more than pay for itself in caught mistakes for the time it costs.

PACE YOURSELF

It's easy to be overwhelmed when you're looking at a page full of questions; your mind is confused and full of random thoughts, and the clock is ticking down faster than you would like. Calm down and maintain the pace that you have set for yourself. Especially as you get down to the last few minutes of the test, don't let the small numbers on the clock make you panic. As long as you are on track by monitoring your pace, you are guaranteed to have time for each question.

DON'T RUSH

It is very easy to make errors when you are in a hurry. Maintaining a fast pace in answering questions is pointless if it makes you miss questions that you would have gotten right otherwise. Test writers like to include distracting information and wrong answers that seem right. Taking a little extra time to avoid careless mistakes can make all the difference in your test score. Find a pace that allows you to be confident in the answers that you select.

Keep Moving

Panicking will not help you pass the test, so do your best to stay calm and keep moving. Taking deep breaths and going through the answer elimination steps you practiced can help to break through a stress barrier and keep your pace.

Final Notes

The combination of a solid foundation of content knowledge and the confidence that comes from practicing your plan for applying that knowledge is the key to maximizing your performance on test day. As your foundation of content knowledge is built up and strengthened, you'll find that the strategies included in this chapter become more and more effective in helping you quickly sift through the distractions and traps of the test to isolate the correct answer.

Now it's time to move on to the test content chapters of this book, but be sure to keep your goal in mind. As you read, think about how you will be able to apply this information on the test. If you've already seen sample questions for the test and you have an idea of the question format and style, try to come up with questions of your own that you can answer based on what you're reading. This will give you valuable practice applying your knowledge in the same ways you can expect to on test day.

Good luck and good studying!

Verbal Reasoning Test

The Verbal Reasoning portion of the GRE consists of two 30-minute sections, with approximately 20 questions per section.

There are three types of questions on the GRE Verbal Test:

1. Sentence Equivalence
2. Text Completion
3. Reading Comprehension

Sentence Equivalence

We will start our review of the GRE Verbal Test with the Sentence Equivalence questions because they comprise one of the easier parts of the exam, and because the principles that apply to the Sentence Equivalence questions will also apply to the Text Completion questions. In this part of the exam, each question will consist of one sentence, with one blank and six possible answer choices, from which you will have to select <u>two</u> answer choices that *both* correctly complete the sentence. It is important to remember that both of your answer choices MUST be correct, or you will not receive credit for the question: there is no partial credit.

Aside from having to pick two correct answers, instead of one, the format of these questions will be otherwise familiar to you from countless other tests, so it is extremely unlikely that you will be confused. For most students, the only obstacle to success on the Sentence Equivalence questions will be an insufficient vocabulary. However, you can vastly improve your score on these exercises by studying lists of common GRE vocabulary words. In addition, there is a basic approach that you can learn to improve your chances on any questions that you do not fully understand.

The basic approach to these questions is simply to read each sentence, and to insert each of the answer choices into the blank, continuing this process until you identify both correct answers. However, never stop prematurely just because you believe that you have found both answers: continue until you have read all of the answers, or you may get caught up in simple word traps. Also, since you know that the question has to be answered correctly by two answer choices, one step to answering the question will involve identifying synonymous words. However, a common trap is for the test taker to identify synonyms in the list, and then prematurely select those words as the answer, when the selected words do not work well to complete the sentence. Therefore, take your time, be careful, and pay attention to the details! What may seem like the best answer choices, at first, may not appear so after you have read all of the options.

ADJECTIVES GIVE THE ANSWERS AWAY

Words have meaning, and are added to the sentence for a reason. Adjectives, in particular, may be the clue to determining which answer choice is correct.

Example: *The brilliant scientist made several _____ discoveries.*

    A. dull
    B. dazzling

Look at the adjectives first, to help determine which word makes sense. A "*brilliant*" scientist would make "*dazzling*", rather than "*dull*", discoveries. Without that simple adjective, no answer choice is clear.

USE LOGIC

Ask yourself questions about each answer choice to see if they are logical.

Example: *The deep pounding resonance of the drums could be _____ far off in the distance.*

    A. seen
    B. heard

Would resonant pounding be "*seen*" or "*heard*"?

POSITIVE OR NEGATIVE

To begin with, read the sentence carefully. Before you look at the answer choices, see if you can predict the words that will best complete the sentence. This is a good exercise for a couple of reasons. For one, you may occasionally find that your predictions are among the answer choices, whereupon you can be almost positive that these answer choices are correct. At the very least, your predictions will give you some information about the correct answer choices. And, by considering the reasons for your predictions, you can give yourself some hints for discovering the right answers. For instance, imagine that you are confronted with the following sentence: "*After Dale lost all of his savings at blackjack, his wife lambasted him for his _____.*" There are a number of words that could adequately complete this sentence: stupidity, irresponsibility, impecuniousness, and prodigality all make sense. Perhaps none of these words are among the answer choices, but we can still make a few helpful observations. For instance, we can note that all of these words are negative, and that several of them refer to poor care of money. Looking back at the sentence, we can affirm that the correct answers will be words that describe someone who is foolish with money. This should give us an advantage when we begin considering the answer choices.

The primary distinction that you will be making, when you make your predictions, will be between positive and negative words. Although it may be impossible for you to remember the precise definition of a word, you can often remember whether that word has a good or bad connotation. In fact, this is a good distinction for you to remember as you are learning new vocabulary words: if you cannot always remember exactly what a word means, see if you can, at least, remember whether it is positive or negative. In most contexts, you should be able to determine whether a positive or negative word is required.

One of the easiest ways to remember whether a given word is positive or negative is to memorize some of the most common prefixes (prefixes generally modify the meanings of words, while suffixes indicate parts of speech).

Before you take the GRE, you should know the following prefixes by heart:

Prefix	Meaning
a-/an-	without, not; e.g. anemic, amoral
ab-	away (from); e.g. abdicate, abrogate
ad-	to, towards; e.g. advance, administer
ante-	before (in chronology); e.g. antecedent, antebellum
anti-	against; e.g. antihero, antibiotic
com-	with; e.g. companion, committee

16

Mometrix

Prefix	Meaning
contra-/counter-	against, opposed to; e.g. contraceptive, counterproductive
de-	down, away (from); e.g. decline, denigrate
ex-	out (of), upward; e.g. exile, exclude
extra-	beyond, outside; e.g. extraordinary, extrapolate
hyper-	extra, more than normal; e.g. hyperactive, hyperspeed
hypo-	under, less than normal; e.g. hypodermic, hypothermia
in-/im-	without, not; e.g. inaccessible, inappropriate, inconclusive
infra-	below; e.g. infrastructure, infraction
inter-	among, between; e.g. interaction, internecine
intra-	inside, within; e.g. intravenous, intramural
non-	lack of, negation of, absence of; e.g. nonjudgmental, nonaggression
ob-	against, blocking, hiding; e.g. obstructive, obstinate
post-	after, following; e.g. posterior, postdate
pro-	in support of, towards, forward; e.g. provide, propel
re-	again, back; e.g. rewind, restore
sub-	lower, beneath, below; e.g. subdue, subjugate
trans-	across, into a different condition; e.g. transition, translate
ultra-	beyond, an extreme version of; e.g. ultrasound, ultramicroscopic

Learning these common prefixes should help you to decipher the meanings of many of the obscure words that appear on the GRE.

Review Video: Prefixes
Visit mometrix.com/academy and enter code: 361382

TRANSITIONAL WORDS

Watch out for key transitional words! This can include the following: however, but, yet, although, so, because, etc. Transitional words may change the meaning of a sentence, as well as the context of the missing word.

Example: *He is an excellent marksman, but surprisingly, he _____ comes home empty-handed from a hunting trip.*

    A. often
    B. never
    C. rarely

A good shot or marksman would be expected to be a successful hunter. Watch out, though, for the transitional phrase: "*but surprisingly*". It indicates the opposite of what you would expect, which means that this particular marksman must not be a successful hunter. A successful hunter would either "*never*" or "*rarely*" come home empty-handed from a hunt, but an unsuccessful hunter would "*often*" come home empty-handed, making A the correct answer choice.

THE TRAP OF FAMILIARITY

Do not just choose words because you recognize them. On difficult questions, you may only recognize one or two words. However, the GRE does not contain "make-believe" words, so do not mistakenly think that any particular words must be correct just because they are the only words that you recognize. If you do not recognize four words, then focus on the ones that you do recognize. Are they correct? Try your best to determine whether they fit the sentence. If they do,

17

then that is great. But, if they do not, then eliminate them. Each word that you can eliminate will increase your chances of getting the question correct.

THE SYNONYM TRAP

On occasion, synonyms will appear among the answer choices, which, upon superficial analysis, may appear to be the correct answers. However, just because two answers choices are synonymous does not mean that they are in fact the correct answers: the correct answers do not have to be synonymous, and there may be more than one pair of synonymous answer choices. This can easily trap test takers who do not carefully read the sentence to confirm that their answers correctly complete the sentence. Therefore, always make sure to carefully read through both the sentence and the answers. Do not settle on any answer choice prematurely, without reading through all of the options. And, always double-check your answers to make sure that both answers will coherently complete the sentence.

Ultimately, the Sentence Equivalence questions are not intended to be the most challenging part of the GRE. They are primarily meant to test your vocabulary, and to ensure that you can read carefully and thoughtfully. If you study your vocabulary lists diligently, there is no reason why these questions should present much difficulty. Even though it is possible that you will have to confront some unfamiliar words in this section of the exam, you can still give yourself every advantage by confronting the questions in a structured, well-ordered manner. Specifically, you should begin by predicting an appropriate answer, and then use your knowledge of prefixes, suffixes, and context clues to guide your decision.

Text Completion

The objective of the Text Completion questions on the GRE Verbal Test is to evaluate the ability of the test taker to reason as they read through sentences and passages. Skilled readers do not simply absorb information as they read. Instead, they constantly analyze, interpret, and reason their way through passages in order to decipher the message that the author intended to convey. The Text Completion questions test this ability by selectively omitting one to three words from short passages, and then requiring the test taker to pick the most appropriate word for each blank from separate lists, which work together to convey the most coherent meaning for the passage.

The format of the Text Completion questions is fairly simple, and should be familiar to anyone who has done fill-in-the-blank exercises in the past. The directions above the exercise will be as follows:

> *For each blank select one entry from the corresponding column of choices. Fill all blanks in the way that best completes the text.*

Below these directions will be a passage of text from one to five sentences long. There will be one to three blanks in this passage, and below the passage will be a table with three answer choices for each of the blanks in the passage. These blanks will be assigned lower-case Roman numerals (i.e. i, ii, or iii), and you, the test taker, will be required to select one answer choice for each blank. In addition, the answers for each blank are independent of one another, meaning that your selection for one blank should not affect your selection for the others. Moreover, it is important to note that the Text Completion questions are also an all-or-none venture: you will not receive any credit if you do not get *all* of the answers correct.

That being said, there is no reason why this type of question should intimidate you. In fact, once we have discussed the basic approach to the Text Completion questions, you may even look forward to these questions! Let us start by taking a look at a sample passage:

> *The American whaling industry __(i)__ between the War of 1812 and the beginning of the Civil War. During this period, scores of coastal towns launched their own whaling enterprises, hoping to cash in on this __(ii)__ trade. It was then that the whaling industry __(iii)__ its greatest stories of perseverance and courage.*

READ THE PASSAGE ALL OF THE WAY THROUGH

Before you continue on to the answer choices, you should always begin by reading the passage all of the way through, just to acquaint yourself with its general structure. As you make this cursory examination of the text, you might go ahead and identify the parts of speech that will be required for each blank. For instance, in the first sentence, the missing word will describe what the whaling industry *did* during this period; it must therefore be a verb. In the second sentence, an adjective will be required to show exactly what *kind* of trade is being discussed. And, in the third sentence, a verb is necessary to describe again what the industry *did*.

IDENTIFY THE SIGNIFICANT WORDS OR PHRASES

Once you have briefly scanned through the passage, you should focus on any significant words that might give you a clue as to the answer. In the above passage, for instance, the words "*hoping to cash in on*" suggest that the whaling trade was doing well at this point. Other passages may contain words that amplify or reverse the meaning. Consider the following sentence: "*Though he was known to be frugal, Henry managed to _____ his fortune in six months.*" Notice how the word "*though*" reverses what is called for by the blank. If "*though*" were not there, we might be looking a word like *increase*, *maintain*, or *raise*. Instead, however, the appropriate word for this blank could be *lose*, *decrease*, or *spend*! In just this way, you might brainstorm some words that would be appropriate for the blanks in our example passage.

FILL-IN-THE-BLANKS IN THE ORDER EASIEST FOR YOU

An important point to remember about Text Completion questions is that you are not required to fill-in-the-blanks in order. Indeed, in our example passage, it would be difficult for you to find an appropriate word for the first blank without first looking at the other blanks. The second sentence indicates that the American whaling industry was getting larger during this period, so the right choice for the first blank would be a word like *grew* or *blossomed*. In the second sentence, the fact that coastal towns were trying to "*cash in*" suggests that the trade was *lucrative* or *booming*. Clearly, by the time you look at the third sentence, you will be aware that this was a glorious age for the whaling industry, which would therefore have *spawned* or *produced* its greatest legends.

MAKE SURE TO RE-READ THE PASSAGE FOR COHERENCE

After you finish filling-in all of the blanks, quickly read back through the sentence, and make sure that your selections produce a passage that is coherent and grammatically correct. The tone and logic of the passage should remain consistent, even if it is not the most elegant piece of prose ever written. Above all, relax and allow yourself to work slowly and systematically through the Text Completion questions. Once you break them down into their constituent parts, they are easy to handle!

PRACTICE EXAMPLE

Now that we have covered the basics of how to approach the Text Completion questions, let us try another example. Read the following passage carefully, apply the tips that we have learned, and then try your best to answer each blank prior to reading the explanation.

It is commonplace these days for scientists to disregard ethics, and publish research articles that are knowingly full of __(i)__ data. Academia has always had a "publish or perish" environment. However, as the number of scientists competing for limited positions and funding increases with each passing year, the pressure for these scientists to publish articles __(ii)__, promoting some scientists to take drastic measures to keep up. Daily, these issues are discovered to set research back greatly; eventually, one could imagine that __(iii)__.

Example Question Answers.		
Blank (i)	**Blank (ii)**	**Blank (iii)**
(A) falsified	(D) reduces	(G) the system may grind to a halt
(B) well-supported	(E) ceases	(H) falsified data may cure cancer
(C) politically-biased	(F) increases	(I) the system may correct itself

EXPLANATION

The overall tone of this passage is generally cynical regarding the current and future state of the scientific research and publishing environments. Analyzing the passage for words or phrases of significance, one quickly notices the first line: "*It is commonplace these days for scientists to disregard ethics...*" This phrase makes it clear that the remainder of the passage is also likely going to be cynical toward the state of scientific research and publishing. Looking at each blank separately, the second blank appears as though it could be answered based upon the context within the third sentence, while the first and third blanks would require context from the remainder of the passage to adequately answer them. Therefore, let us start with the second blank first.

In the third sentence, the statements that 'competition increases annually', and that "*some scientists... take drastic measures to keep up*", suggest that the "*pressure for these scientists to publish articles*" likely also increases. Looking at the answer choices, our initial answer is among the available options, and is likely the correct answer. The remaining answers simply do not logically complete the sentence: in an increasingly intense work environment, one would not expect that the pressure on the scientists "*decreases*" or "*ceases*". Therefore, we will accept "*increases*" as the answer for the second blank.

Based upon the statement in the first sentence – that scientists commonly disregard ethics; we can quickly eliminate "*well-supported*" from our answer pool for the first blank: scientists who disregard ethics would not likely be publishing well-supported data within the same sentence. The remaining two choices: "*falsified*" and "*politically-biased*", are both equally possible without further context. Having determined the answer for the second blank, we could easily surmise that the 'increased pressure' that these unethical scientists are subjected to would drive them to publish articles that are full of "*falsified*" data. Alternatively, for the unethical data to be "*politically-biased*", we would expect for the context of the remainder of the passage to suggest some form of ulterior motive or advantage gained from such political bias, which it does not. Thus, the answer for the first blank is "*falsified*".

Finally, for the third blank, we can quickly eliminate the second option: it would be unlikely for falsified data to lead to a dramatic cure for any ailment. Without context, the remaining two answer choices would seem equally possible. However, given the cynical tone of the remainder of the passage, we can now conclude that the author likely does not believe that "*the system may correct itself*" without some overhaul of the system by external forces. Therefore, the answer to the third blank is "*the system may grind to a halt*".

Putting all of these together, our answers for this passage are as follows:

  i. (A) falsified
  ii. (F) increases
  iii. (G) the system may grind to a halt

As it turns out, this is the correct answer. However, again, keep in mind that, if any of these three answers is incorrect, then the entire question would be deemed incorrect: there is no partial credit. So, always remember to double-check your final answer prior to moving on, and make sure that the final passage is coherent and grammatically correct. By incorporating our answers into the example passage, we can see that the final passage is both coherent and grammatically correct:

> *It is commonplace these days for scientists to disregard ethics, and publish research articles that are knowingly full of (i) (A) falsified data. Academia has always had a "publish or perish" environment. However, as the number of scientists competing for limited positions and funding increases with each passing year, the pressure for these scientists to publish articles (ii) (F) increases , promoting some scientists to take drastic measures to keep up. Daily, these issues are discovered to set research back greatly; eventually, one could imagine that (iii) (G) the system may grind to a halt .*

Reading Comprehension

The Reading Comprehension questions are the component of the GRE Verbal Test that requires the most work. Each Reading Comprehension question will be based upon a passage that ranges between one and several paragraphs. In addition, the exam will contain approximately ten passages, the majority of which will consist of one paragraph, while only one or two will contain multiple paragraphs. These passages will be drawn from the following content areas: biology, physical science, social science, and the humanities. Typically, approximately half of the questions on the GRE Verbal Test will be based upon passages, with one to six questions based upon any given passage. These questions will primarily be of four basic types: main idea, detail, tone, or extending the author's reasoning, each of which will call for a slightly different approach, as will be discussed shortly. The answer format for these questions will vary: most will be standard multiple-choice questions, in which you will be required to select a single correct answer, but some will require for you to either choose more than one correct answer, or to select a sentence from the passage. Also, regardless of whether you are taking the exam on a computer or on paper, you will be able to read back through the passages as much as you like, and all of the information that will be required to answer the questions will be found in the passages: you will not need any outside information or experience to answer the questions. Now, before we take a further look at the types of Reading Comprehension questions, let us discuss how you can prepare for the three types of passages.

The biological and physical science passages are probably the most daunting for the majority of test takers. Those students, whose undergraduate careers did not include a great deal of hard science, may be taken aback by the rigid structure and torrent of facts in a science passage. Just remember that the questions on the GRE will not require any outside knowledge. It is also good to keep in mind that you do not need to memorize the information in the passage, since you will be able to refer to the text as much as you like. The science passages on the GRE will be either specific or general. A specific science passage describes a particular study or set of research data, usually without mentioning any ideas or ramifications outside of the boundaries of the study. A specific passage will be akin to an article in a scientific journal. A general science passage, on the other hand, will be more like an article in a scientific magazine. That is, it will describe a science-related topic in a manner that is more accessible to a general audience. It is typical for a general science article to spend some time discussing the possible consequences of research, or on general theories that have arisen out of recent studies. Regardless of whether the science passage on your GRE is specific or general, try to pay attention to the main themes of the passage without getting mired in excessive details. The questions that follow a science passage will most likely pertain to the elements of the passage that are most obvious to a reader with a non-science background.

The second content area, from which the Reading Comprehension passages may be drawn, is the social sciences. The social sciences include sociology, psychology, history, business, and anthropology, among others. By and large, the social science passages will break down in a manner similar to other science passages, being either specific or general. One difference is that the authors of the GRE will expect you to be a little bit better at extrapolating and making inferences based on the information in a social science passage. The authors assume that your common sense will enable you to evaluate a social science passage with more insight. For this reason, on a social science passage, you are more likely to be asked to extend the reasoning of the passage, or to describe the attitude of the author.

The third and final content area, from which the Reading Comprehension questions are drawn, is the humanities. The humanities are any of the so-called arts, including drama, literature, philosophy, music, and painting. However, you are unlikely to encounter primary sources on the GRE. Instead, reading passages from the humanities will most likely be works of criticism, in which the author reflects on a particular work or artist. (Remember that, in the humanities, the word criticism does not necessarily imply a negative opinion: some criticism heaps praise on its subject.) These passages should be easy to read and understand, and the questions that follow are likely to require inferences and some independent thought. Also, because these passages are not meant to be objective, you are more likely to be asked to evaluate the attitude and perspective of the author.

MAIN IDEA QUESTIONS

The first, and most basic, type of Reading Comprehension question is the one that asks you to define the main idea of the passage. This question may arrive in any of a few different forms. The question may ask you for the "the best summary", the "salient point", or the "overarching theme" of the passage. There is no need to be baffled by this language: this is a main idea question. As you no doubt have learned by now, the main idea of a passage is most likely to appear in either the first or the last sentence. As you are reading a passage for the first time, pay special attention to the beginning and end. Whether the main idea is offered first or last will depend on the type of passage: expository passages tend to give a main idea first, and then spend the rest of the sentences defending it, while critical or argumentative essays will often begin with a set of loose facts, and end with a summarizing conclusion. In any case, be prepared to refer back to the text in search of the main idea.

On occasion, the authors of the GRE will try to fool you by asking you to provide the main idea of a specific part of the passage, rather than of the passage as a whole. Similarly, they may try to confuse you with answer choices that are true, without being the main idea of the passage. For this reason, it is imperative that you read the question carefully, and not assume that the first or last sentence of the paragraph is the main idea. The main idea is not just any true statement that is contained within the passage: it is the idea that most effectively summarizes the entire passage.

Review Video: Topics and Main Ideas
Visit mometrix.com/academy and enter code: 407801

SPECIFIC DETAIL QUESTIONS

It is quite likely that a few of the questions will ask you to recall specific details from the passage. This would appear to be the easiest kind of question to answer, but many students go astray by relying on memory instead of scrolling back up to find the pertinent details in the passage. As mentioned above, both the computer and paper versions of the GRE allow you to refer to the text at will. Take advantage of this freedom. Also, remember that specific questions are likely to have specific answers, just as general questions are likely to have general answers. In other words, if the question asks for the identity of a concept, then the answer probably will not be a specific piece of data.

AUTHOR'S FEELING QUESTIONS

A more subtle form of questioning requires you to speculate on the author's attitude. As with the main idea question, this kind of question can take a number of different forms: it may ask you to describe the "tone", "opinion", "feeling", or "mood" of the author or passage. All of these questions are essentially asking you to assess how the author feels about his or her topic. In order to answer such a question, you will have to pay attention to the specific language that is used by the author, and the point of view that the language conveys. For instance, if the author is describing a small person, he or she would create a sharply different tone by using the word puny, rather than would be created by using the word petite: puny suggests a shriveled, scrawny individual, while petite conjures daintiness and delicacy. It may take a little bit of practice before you habitually notice these shades of meaning, but you should try to be conscious of the ways in which language can be used to subtly indicate attitude.

When dealing with questions of tone, you should also consider the genre of the passage. For instance, specific science passages are almost always written in an objective, nonjudgmental tone, regardless of whether in the biological, physical, or social sciences. These passages will rarely demonstrate a strong opinion, so you should avoid any answer choices that suggest a positive or negative view on the part of the author. Critical essays in the humanities, on the other hand, will often be quite opinionated. Even general passages on the sciences may evince a clear positive or negative disposition. However, the ETS generally avoids using passages that are violently opinionated or controversial. Any answer choices that suggest that the author holds an opinion that could be considered radical or offensive are most likely incorrect.

AUTHOR'S REASONING QUESTIONS

The final type of question that you may encounter on the GRE is one that asks you to extend the author's reasoning. Put another way, this question will require you to consider the information provided in the passage, and then use this information to consider a problem not mentioned in the passage. For instance, a specific science passage, regarding the migratory patterns of a certain predatory bird, might ask you to consider the effects of these migrations on the populations of rodents in various regions. Even if the passage has not mentioned rodents up to this point, you should be able to guess that more rodents will be killed when the predatory birds are in the area. The most common problem students have with questions that ask them to extend the reasoning of the passage is that they attempt to find the answer explicitly in the passage. Remember that, even though all of the information that is needed to answer every question can be found in the text, some questions will require you to do some independent thinking.

SKIMMING

When you begin reading, your first task is to answer the following question: "What is the topic of the selection?" This can be answered best by quickly skimming the passage for the general idea, stopping only to read the first sentence of each paragraph. A paragraph's first sentence is usually the main topic sentence, and it gives you a summary of the content of the paragraph.

Once you have skimmed the passage, reading only the first sentences, you will have a general idea of what the passage is about, as well as what the expected topic is for each paragraph.

Each question will contain clues as to where to find the answer in the passage. Do not just randomly search through the passage for the correct answer to each question; search scientifically. Find key words or ideas in the question that are going to either contain or be near the correct answer. These are typically nouns, verbs, numbers, or phrases in the question that will probably be duplicated in the passage. Once you have identified the key words or ideas, quickly skim the passage to find where those key words or ideas appear. The correct answer choice will be nearby.

Example: *What caused Martin to suddenly return to Paris?*

The key word is "*Paris*". Skim the passage to quickly find where this word appears. The answer will be close by that word.

However, sometimes, key words in the question are not repeated in the passage. In those cases, search for the general idea of the question.

Example: *Which of the following was the psychological impact of the author's childhood upon the remainder of his life?*

The key words are "*childhood*" or "*psychological*". While searching for those words, be alert for other words or phrases that have similar meaning, such as "emotional effect" or "mental", which could be used in the passage, rather than the exact word "*psychological*".

Numbers or years can be particularly good key words to skim for, as they stand out from the rest of the text.

Example: *Which of the following best describes the influence of Monet's work in the 20th century?*

"*20th century*" contains numbers, and will easily stand out from the rest of the text. Use "*20th*" as the key word to skim for in the passage.

Other good key words may be in quotation marks. These identify a word or phrase that is copied directly from the passage. In those cases, the words in quotation marks are exactly duplicated in the passage.

Example: *In her college years, what was meant by Margaret's "drive for excellence"?*

"*Drive for excellence*" is a direct quote from the passage, and should be easy to find.

BEWARE OF DIRECTLY-QUOTED ANSWERS

Once you have quickly found the correct section of the passage in which to find the answer, focus on the answer choices. Sometimes, a choice will repeat word-for-word a portion of the passage near

24

the answer.ⁱ However, beware of such duplication: it may be a trap! More than likely, the correct choice will paraphrase, or summarize, the related portion of the passage, rather than being a direct quote.

TRUTH DOES NOT EQUAL CORRECTNESS

For the answers that you think are correct, read them carefully, and make sure that they answer the question. An answer can be factually correct, but it MUST answer the question that is asked. Additionally, two answers can both be seemingly correct, so be sure to read all of the answer choices, and make sure that you select the one that *best* answers the question.

WHEN THERE IS NO KEY WORD

Sometimes, it may be difficult to identify a good key work in the question to skim for in the passage, or the question may not have a key word.

Example: *Which of the following would the author of this passage likely agree with?*

In these cases, look for key words in the answer choices, and then skim the passage to find where the answer choice occurs. By skimming to find where to look, you can minimize the time required. Oftentimes, the answer choices will all be found in the same paragraph, which can quickly narrow your search.

> **Review Video: When There's No Keyword**
> Visit mometrix.com/academy and enter code: 312791

PARAGRAPH FOCUS

Focus on the first sentence of each paragraph, which is generally the most important sentence. The main topic of the paragraph can usually be found there.

Once you have read the first sentence of the paragraph, you will have a general idea of what each paragraph will be about. As you read the questions, try to determine which paragraph has the answer. Paragraphs have a concise topic, and the answer should either be obviously there, or obviously not there. It will save time if you can jump straight to the paragraph, so try to remember what you learned from the first sentences.

Example: *The first paragraph is about poets; the second paragraph is about poetry.*

If a question asks about poetry, then you would search for the answer in the second paragraph.

The main idea of a passage is typically spread across all, or most, of its paragraphs. Whereas the main idea of a paragraph may be completely different than the main idea of the very next paragraph, the main idea of a passage affects all of the paragraphs in one form or another.

Example: *What is the main idea of the passage?*

For each answer choice, try to see how many paragraphs are related. It can help you to count how many sentences are affected by each choice, but it is best to see how many paragraphs are affected by the choice. Typically, the answer choices will include incorrect choices that are main ideas of individual paragraphs, but not of the entire passage. That is why it is crucial to choose ideas that are supported by the most paragraphs possible.

ELIMINATE CHOICES

Some choices can be quickly eliminated. If an answer choice is: "*Andy Warhol lived there*", then is "*Andy Warhol*" even mentioned in the article? If not, then quickly eliminate it.

When trying to answer a question, such as "*the passage indicates all of the following EXCEPT*", quickly skim the passage, and search for references to each choice. If the reference exists, scratch it off as a choice. Similar choices may be crossed-off simultaneously if they are close enough.

Watch for answers that are similarly worded. Since only one answer can be correct, if there are two answers that appear to mean the same thing, then they must BOTH be incorrect, and can be eliminated.

Example Answer Choices:

    A. changing values and attitudes
    B. a large population of mobile or uprooted people

These answer choices are similar in that they both describe a fluid culture. Because of their similarity, they can be linked together. And, since the question can have only one answer; they can also be eliminated together.

CONTEXTUAL CLUES

Look for contextual clues. An answer can be right, but incorrect. The contextual clues will help you to find the answer that is the most right, and is correct. Understand the context in which a phrase is stated.

When asked for the implied meaning of a statement made in the passage, immediately find the statement, and then read the context. Also, look for an answer choice that has a similar phrase to the statement in question.

Example: *In the passage, what is implied by the phrase: "Churches have become more or less part of the furniture"?*

Find an answer choice that is similar to, or describes, the phrase "*part of the furniture*", as that is the key phrase in the question. "*Part of the furniture*" is a saying that means something is fixed, immovable, or set in their ways. Since those are all similar ways of saying "*part of the furniture*", the correct answer choice will probably include a similar rewording of the expression.

Example: *Why was John described as being "morally desperate"?*

The answer will probably have some sort of definition of morals in it. Morals refers to a code of right and wrong behavior, so the correct answer choice will likely have words that have a similar meaning.

FACT/OPINION

Remember that answer choices that are facts will typically have no ambiguous words. For example, how long is a long time? What defines an ordinary person? These ambiguous words, "long" and "ordinary", should not be in a factual statement. However, if all of the choices have ambiguous words, then go to the context of the passage.

Often, a factual statement will be set out as a research finding.

Example: *"The scientist found that the eye reacts quickly to changes in light."*

Opinions may be set out in the context of words like thought, believed, understood, or wished.

Example: *"He thought that the Yankees should have won the World Series."*

Final Warnings

HEDGE PHRASES REVISITED

Once again, watch out for critical "hedge" phrases, such as "likely", "may", "can", "often", "will often", "almost", "mostly", "usually", "generally", "rarely", "sometimes", etc. Question writers insert these hedge phrases to cover every possibility. Often, an answer will be wrong simply because it leaves no room for exception.

Example: *Animals live longer in cold places than animals in warm places.*

This answer choice is wrong because there are exceptions in which certain warm climate animals live longer. This answer choice leaves no possibility for exception. It states that every animal species in cold places live longer than animal species in warm places. Correct answer choices will typically have a key hedge word to leave room for exceptions.

Example: *In severe cold, a polar bear cub is likely to survive longer than an adult polar bear.*

This answer choice is correct because, not only does the passage imply that younger animals survive better in the cold, but it also allows for exceptions to exist. The use of the word *"likely"* leaves room for cases in which a polar bear cub might not survive longer than the adult polar bear.

WORD USAGE QUESTIONS

When asked how a word is used in the passage, make sure not to use your existing knowledge of the word. The question is being asked precisely because there is some strange or unusual usage of the word in the passage. Go to the passage, and use contextual clues to determine the answer. Do not simply use the popular definition that you already know.

SWITCHBACK WORDS

Stay alert for "switchbacks". These are the words and phrases that are frequently used to alert you to shifts in thought. The most common switchback word is "but". Others include "although", "however", "nevertheless", "on the other hand", "even though", "while", "in spite of", "despite", and "regardless of".

AVOID "FACT TRAPS"

Once you know which paragraph the answer will be in, focus on that paragraph. However, do not get distracted by a choice that is factually true about the paragraph. Your search is for the answer choice that answers the question, which may be about a tiny aspect in the paragraph. Stay focused, and do not fall for an answer that describes the larger picture of the paragraph. Always go back to the question, and make sure that you are choosing an answer choice that actually answers the question; not just a true statement.

Quantitative Reasoning Test

The Quantitative Reasoning portion of the GRE consists of two 35-minute sections, with approximately 20 questions per section.

The GRE Quantitative Test seems to generate the most anxiety among prospective test takers. For individuals hoping to enter graduate programs in sociology or history, it may seem unfair to be tested on their skill with numbers. Unfortunately, the Quantitative Test is here to stay. The good news is that most experts consider the mathematics that is included on the GRE to be significantly less difficult than the math on the SAT. Indeed, ETS has developed this portion of the exam to be at approximately a ninth-grade level. Therefore, if you did not take much math as an undergraduate, do not worry. Studying for the Quantitative Test is primarily a matter of learning the best strategies for solving the different types of questions, and then brushing up on your junior high and high school math.

There are four types of questions on the GRE Quantitative Test:

1. Quantitative Comparison
2. Problem Solving – Multiple Choice – Select One Answer Choice
3. Problem Solving – Multiple Choice – Select One or More Answer Choice
4. Problem Solving – Numerical Entry

Each question will either be based upon discrete problem sets, or will be part of a group of questions that are collectively based upon data presented in tables or graphs, called data interpretation sets. The Quantitative Comparison questions will present two different quantities or equations, and will ask you to compare the two in order to determine if one is greater than the other, if they are equal to one another, or if the relationship cannot be determined. The three different types of Problem Solving questions will all be similar in nature, requiring you to determine a specific answer based upon a problem or data interpretation set, but will differ in the style of answer required to answer each type of question. Specifically, there will be two different types of Multiple Choice questions: one will require you to select one correct answer, while the other will require you to select one or more correct answers. It is important to note that, while the 'one or more correct answer choice' questions will indicate that more than one answer choice is *possible*; these questions may not indicate exactly how many answer choices are possible. Finally, the Numerical Entry questions will differ from the Multiple Choice questions in that no answers will be provided. Instead, the test taker will have to calculate a specific answer for the question, end then manually enter their answer into a box (or more than one box in the case of a fraction: one box for the numerator, and one box for the denominator).

If you are concerned about your arithmetic, a calculator WILL be allowed on the GRE: on the computer-based exam, a basic on-screen calculator will be provided, and on the paper-based exam, a basic hand-held calculator will be provided. Scratch paper and pencils will also be made available. In order to ensure the accuracy of your calculations, you should use this scratch paper as much as you can, and use the calculator only for tedious calculations, such as long division. Do not try to solve complicated problems in your head, and do not use the calculator for long strings of calculations without keeping track of them on paper: write your calculations down to get a visual sense of your work-in-progress, to leave your mind free to work, and to keep a record of your units in order to ensure that your calculations are on track. The importance of scratch paper is true for the Quantitative Comparison questions, as well as the Problem Solving questions. On the Problem

Solving questions, you should use the paper to solve each problem both forward and backward. For instance, on a question that asks you to solve for a specific variable, you should solve for the variable, and then plug that variable back into the original equation in order to make sure that it works. By double-checking your work in this manner, you can prevent careless mistakes from lowering your score.

Quantitative Comparison

For these questions, you will have to determine a relationship between two quantities: A and B. You will be asked whether A is greater, B is greater, A is equal to B, or the relationship cannot be determined.

First, understand the directions so that you do not have to waste precious time referring back to them. For Quantitative Comparison questions, the possible answers are as follows:

1. If the quantity in Column A is greater
2. If the quantity in Column B is greater
3. If the two quantities are equal
4. If the relationship cannot be determined based upon the information provided

Many first-time test takers become overwhelmed by finding the Quantitative Comparison questions unnecessarily complex. However, there is no reason to fear these questions any more than Problem Solving questions: the operations that you will be required to perform in the Quantitative Comparison questions are no different from those found in the Problem Solving questions. The best way to demystify Quantitative Comparison questions is to work through them in an orderly and deliberate manner. Specifically, you should always solve first for the value in Column A, solve next for the value in Column B, and then compare the two.

Do not attempt to compare the two columns until you have either converted them into terms that can be compared, or have determined that it is impossible to make the comparison.

Numbers and Operations

NUMBERS AND THEIR CLASSIFICATIONS

Numbers are the basic building blocks of mathematics. Specific features of numbers are identified by the following terms:

- Integers – The set of positive and negative numbers, including zero. Integers do not include fractions $\left(\frac{1}{3}\right)$, decimals (0.56), or mixed numbers $\left(7\frac{3}{4}\right)$.
- Even number – Any integer that can be divided by 2 without leaving a remainder. For example: 2, 4, 6, 8, and so on.
- Odd number – Any integer that cannot be divided evenly by 2. For example: 3, 5, 7, 9, and so on.
- Decimal number – a number that uses a decimal point to show the part of the number that is less than one. Example: 1.234.
- Decimal point – a symbol used to separate the ones place from the tenths place in decimals or dollars from cents in currency.
- Decimal place – the position of a number to the right of the decimal point. In the decimal 0.123, the 1 is in the first place to the right of the decimal point, indicating tenths; the 2 is in the second place, indicating hundredths; and the 3 is in the third place, indicating thousandths.

The decimal, or base 10, system is a number system that uses ten different digits (0, 1, 2, 3, 4, 5, 6, 7, 8, 9). An example of a number system that uses something other than ten digits is the binary, or base 2, number system, used by computers, which uses only the numbers 0 and 1. It is thought that the decimal system originated because people had only their 10 fingers for counting.

> **Review Video: Numbers and Their Classifications**
> Visit mometrix.com/academy and enter code: 461071

OPERATIONS

There are four basic mathematical operations:

- Addition increases the value of one quantity by the value of another quantity. Example: 2 + 4 = 6; 8 + 9 = 17. The result is called the sum. With addition, the order does not matter. 4 + 2 = 2 + 4.
- Subtraction is the opposite operation to addition; it decreases the value of one quantity by the value of another quantity. Example: 6 – 4 = 2; 17 – 8 = 9. The result is called the difference. Note that with subtraction, the order does matter. 6 – 4 ≠ 4 – 6.
- Multiplication can be thought of as repeated addition. One number tells how many times to add the other number to itself. Example: 3 × 2 (three times two) = 2 + 2 + 2 = 6. With multiplication, the order does not matter. 2 × 3 (or 3 + 3) = 3 × 2 (or 2 + 2 + 2).
- Division is the opposite operation to multiplication; one number tells us how many parts to divide the other number into. Example: 20 ÷ 4 = 5; if 20 is split into 4 equal parts, each part is 5. With division, the order of the numbers does matter. 20 ÷ 4 ≠ 4 ÷ 20.

An exponent is a superscript number placed next to another number at the top right. It indicates how many times the base number is to be multiplied by itself. Exponents provide a shorthand way to write what would be a longer mathematical expression. Example: $a^2 = a \times a$; $2^4 = 2 \times 2 \times 2 \times 2$. A number with an exponent of 2 is said to be "squared," while a number with an exponent of 3 is said to be "cubed." The value of a number raised to an exponent is called its power. So, 8^4 is read as "8 to the 4th power," or "8 raised to the power of 4." A negative exponent is the same as the reciprocal of a positive exponent. Example: $a^{-2} = 1/a^2$.

Parentheses are used to designate which operations should be done first when there are multiple operations. Example: $4 - (2 + 1) = 1$; the parentheses tell us that we must add 2 and 1, and then subtract the sum from 4, rather than subtracting 2 from 4 and then adding 1 (this would give us an answer of 3).

Order of Operations is a set of rules that dictates the order in which we must perform each operation in an expression so that we will evaluate it accurately. If we have an expression that includes multiple different operations, Order of Operations tells us which operations to do first. The most common mnemonic for Order of Operations is PEMDAS, or "Please Excuse My Dear Aunt Sally." PEMDAS stands for Parentheses, Exponents, Multiplication, Division, Addition, Subtraction. It is important to understand that multiplication and division have equal precedence, as do addition and subtraction, so those pairs of operations are simply worked from left to right in order.

Example: Evaluate the expression $5 + 20 \div 4 \times (2 + 3)^2 - 6$ using the correct order of operations.

P: Perform the operations inside the parentheses, $(2 + 3) = 5$.

E: Simplify the exponents, $(5)^2 = 25$.

The equation now looks like this: $5 + 20 \div 4 \times 25 - 6$.

MD: Perform multiplication and division from left to right, $20 \div 4 = 5$; then $5 \times 25 = 125$.

The equation now looks like this: $5 + 125 - 6$.

AS: Perform addition and subtraction from left to right, $5 + 125 = 130$; then $130 - 6 = 124$.

Review Video: <u>Order of Operations</u>
Visit mometrix.com/academy and enter code: 259675

The laws of exponents are as follows:

1. Any number to the power of 1 is equal to itself: $a^1 = a$.
2. The number 1 raised to any power is equal to 1: $1^n = 1$.
3. Any number raised to the power of 0 is equal to 1: $a^0 = 1$.
4. Add exponents to multiply powers of the same base number: $a^n \times a^m = a^{n+m}$.
5. Subtract exponents to divide powers of the same number; that is $a^n \div a^m = a^{n-m}$.
6. Multiply exponents to raise a power to a power: $(a^n)^m = a^{n \times m}$.
7. If multiplied or divided numbers inside parentheses are collectively raised to a power, this is the same as each individual term being raised to that power: $(a \times b)^n = a^n \times b^n$; $(a \div b)^n = a^n \div b^n$.

Note: Exponents do not have to be integers. Fractional or decimal exponents follow all the rules above as well. Example: $5^{\frac{1}{4}} \times 5^{\frac{3}{4}} = 5^{\frac{1}{4}+\frac{3}{4}} = 5^1 = 5$.

Review Video: <u>Laws of Exponents</u>
Visit mometrix.com/academy and enter code: 532558

A root, such as a square root, is another way of writing a fractional exponent. Instead of using a superscript, roots use the radical symbol ($\sqrt{}$) to indicate the operation. A radical will have a number underneath the bar, and may sometimes have a number in the upper left: $\sqrt[n]{a}$, read as "the nth root of a." The relationship between radical notation and exponent notation can be described by this equation: $\sqrt[n]{a} = a^{1/n}$. The two special cases of n = 2 and n = 3 are called square roots and cube roots. If there is no number to the upper left, it is understood to be a square root (n = 2). Nearly all of the roots you encounter will be square roots. A square root is the same as a number raised to the one-half power. When we say that a is the square root of b (a = $\sqrt{b}$), we mean that a multiplied by itself equals b: (a × a = b).

A perfect square is a number that has an integer for its square root. There are 10 perfect squares from 1 to 100: 1, 4, 9, 16, 25, 36, 49, 64, 81, 100 (the squares of integers 1 through 10).

Scientific notation is a way of writing large numbers in a shorter form. The form $a \times 10^n$ is used in scientific notation, where a is greater than or equal to 1, but less than 10, and n is the number of places the decimal must move to get from the original number to a. Example: The number 230,400,000 is cumbersome to write. To write the value in scientific notation, place a decimal point between the first and second numbers, and include all digits through the last non-zero digit (a = 2.304). To find the appropriate power of 10, count the number of places the decimal point had to move (n = 8). The number is positive if the decimal moved to the left, and negative if it moved to the right. We can then write 230,400,000 as 2.304×10^8. If we look instead at the number 0.00002304, we have the same value for a, but this time the decimal moved 5 places to the right (n = -5). Thus, 0.00002304 can be written as 2.304×10^{-5}. Using this notation makes it simple to compare very large or very small numbers. By comparing exponents, it is easy to see that 3.28×10^4 is smaller than 1.51×10^5, because 4 is less than 5.

FACTORS AND MULTIPLES

Factors are numbers that are multiplied together to obtain a product. For example, in the equation 2 × 3 = 6, the numbers 2 and 3 are factors. A prime number has only two factors (1 and itself), but other numbers can have many factors.

> **Review Video: Factors**
> Visit mometrix.com/academy and enter code: 920086

A common factor is a number that divides exactly into two or more other numbers. For example, the factors of 12 are 1, 2, 3, 4, 6, and 12, while the factors of 15 are 1, 3, 5, and 15. The common factors of 12 and 15 are 1 and 3.

A prime factor is also a prime number. Therefore, the prime factors of 12 are 2 and 3. For 15, the prime factors are 3 and 5.

The greatest common factor (GCF) is the largest number that is a factor of two or more numbers. For example, the factors of 15 are 1, 3, 5, and 15; the factors of 35 are 1, 5, 7, and 35. Therefore, the greatest common factor of 15 and 35 is 5.

The least common multiple (LCM) is the smallest number that is a multiple of two or more numbers. For example, the multiples of 3 include 3, 6, 9, 12, 15, etc.; the multiples of 5 include 5, 10, 15, 20, etc. Therefore, the least common multiple of 3 and 5 is 15.

> **Review Video: Multiples**
> Visit mometrix.com/academy and enter code: 626738

FRACTIONS, PERCENTAGES, AND RELATED CONCEPTS

A fraction is a number that is expressed as one integer written above another integer, with a dividing line between them $\left(\frac{x}{y}\right)$. It represents the quotient of the two numbers "x divided by y." It can also be thought of as x out of y equal parts.

The top number of a fraction is called the numerator, and it represents the number of parts under consideration. The 1 in $\frac{1}{4}$ means that 1 part out of the whole is being considered in the calculation. The bottom number of a fraction is called the denominator, and it represents the total number of equal parts. The 4 in $\frac{1}{4}$ means that the whole consists of 4 equal parts. A fraction cannot have a denominator of zero; this is referred to as "undefined."

Fractions can be manipulated by multiplying or dividing (but not adding or subtracting) both the numerator and denominator by the same number, without changing the value of the fraction. If you divide both numbers by a common factor, you are reducing or simplifying the fraction. Two fractions that have the same value, but are expressed differently are known as equivalent fractions. For example, $\frac{2}{10}, \frac{3}{15}, \frac{4}{20}$, and $\frac{5}{25}$ are all equivalent fractions. They can also all be reduced or simplified to $\frac{1}{5}$.

When two fractions are manipulated so that they have the same denominator, this is known as finding a common denominator. The number chosen to be that common denominator should be the least common multiple of the two original denominators. Example: $\frac{3}{4}$ and $\frac{5}{6}$; the least common multiple of 4 and 6 is 12. Manipulating to achieve the common denominator: $\frac{3}{4} = \frac{9}{12}$; $\frac{5}{6} = \frac{10}{12}$.

If two fractions have a common denominator, they can be added or subtracted simply by adding or subtracting the two numerators and retaining the same denominator. Example: $\frac{1}{2} + \frac{1}{4} = \frac{2}{4} + \frac{1}{4} = \frac{3}{4}$. If the two fractions do not already have the same denominator, one or both of them must be manipulated to achieve a common denominator before they can be added or subtracted.

Two fractions can be multiplied by multiplying the two numerators to find the new numerator and the two denominators to find the new denominator. Example: $\frac{1}{3} \times \frac{2}{3} = \frac{1 \times 2}{3 \times 3} = \frac{2}{9}$.

Two fractions can be divided flipping the numerator and denominator of the second fraction and then proceeding as though it were a multiplication. Example: $\frac{2}{3} \div \frac{3}{4} = \frac{2}{3} \times \frac{4}{3} = \frac{8}{9}$.

A fraction whose denominator is greater than its numerator is known as a proper fraction, while a fraction whose numerator is greater than its denominator is known as an improper fraction. Proper fractions have values less than one and improper fractions have values greater than one.

A mixed number is a number that contains both an integer and a fraction. Any improper fraction can be rewritten as a mixed number. Example: $\frac{8}{3} = \frac{6}{3} + \frac{2}{3} = 2 + \frac{2}{3} = 2\frac{2}{3}$. Similarly, any mixed number can be rewritten as an improper fraction. Example: $1\frac{3}{5} = 1 + \frac{3}{5} = \frac{5}{5} + \frac{3}{5} = \frac{8}{5}$.

Review Video: Fractions
Visit mometrix.com/academy and enter code: 262335

33

Percentages can be thought of as fractions that are based on a whole of 100; that is, one whole is equal to 100%. The word percent means "per hundred." Fractions can be expressed as percents by finding equivalent fractions with a denomination of 100. Example: $\frac{7}{10} = \frac{70}{100} = 70\%; \frac{1}{4} = \frac{25}{100} = 25\%$.

To express a percentage as a fraction, divide the percentage number by 100 and reduce the fraction to its simplest possible terms. Example: $60\% = \frac{60}{100} = \frac{3}{5}; 96\% = \frac{96}{100} = \frac{24}{25}$.

Converting decimals to percentages and percentages to decimals is as simple as moving the decimal point. To convert from a decimal to a percent, move the decimal point two places to the right. To convert from a percent to a decimal, move it two places to the left. Example: 0.23 = 23%; 5.34 = 534%; 0.007 = 0.7%; 700% = 7.00; 86% = 0.86; 0.15% = 0.0015.

It may be helpful to remember that the percentage number will always be larger than the equivalent decimal number.

A percentage problem can be presented three main ways: (1) Find what percentage of some number another number is. Example: What percentage of 40 is 8? (2) Find what number is some percentage of a given number. Example: What number is 20% of 40? (3) Find what number another number is a given percentage of. Example: What number is 8 20% of? The three components in all of these cases are the same: a whole (W), a part (P), and a percentage (%). These are related by the equation: P = W × %. This is the form of the equation you would use to solve problems of type (2). To solve types (1) and (3), you would use these two forms: % = P/W and W = P/%.

The thing that frequently makes percentage problems difficult is that they are most often also word problems, so a large part of solving them is figuring out which quantities are what. Example: In a school cafeteria, 7 students choose pizza, 9 choose hamburgers, and 4 choose tacos. Find the percentage that chooses tacos. To find the whole, you must first add all of the parts: 7 + 9 + 4 = 20. The percentage can then be found by dividing the part by the whole (% = P/W): $\frac{4}{20} = \frac{20}{100} = 20\%$.

> **Review Video: Percentages**
> Visit mometrix.com/academy and enter code: 141911

A ratio is a comparison of two quantities in a particular order. Example: If there are 14 computers in a lab, and the class has 20 students, there is a student to computer ratio of 20 to 14, commonly written as 20:14.

A proportion is a relationship between two quantities that dictates how one changes when the other changes. A direct proportion describes a relationship in which a quantity increases by a set amount for every increase in the other quantity, or decreases by that same amount for every decrease in the other quantity. Example: For every 1 sheet cake, 18 people can be served cake. The number of sheet cakes, and the number of people that can be served from them is directly proportional.

Inverse proportion is a relationship in which an increase in one quantity is accompanied by a decrease in the other, or vice versa. Example: the time required for a car trip decreases as the speed increases, and increases as the speed decreases, so the time required is inversely proportional to the speed of the car.

HANDLING POSITIVE AND NEGATIVE NUMBERS

A precursor to working with negative numbers is understanding what absolute values are. A number's *Absolute Value* is simply the distance away from zero a number is on the number line. The absolute value of a number is always positive and is written $|x|$.

When adding signed numbers, if the signs are the same simply add the absolute values of the addends and apply the original sign to the sum. For example, $(+4) + (+8) = +12$ and $(-4) + (-8) = -12$. When the original signs are different, take the absolute values of the addends and subtract the smaller value from the larger value, then apply the original sign of the larger value to the difference. For instance, $(+4) + (-8) = -4$ and $(-4) + (+8) = +4$.

For subtracting signed numbers, change the sign of the number after the minus symbol and then follow the same rules used for addition. For example, $(+4) - (+8) = (+4) + (-8) = -4$.

If the signs are the same the product is positive when multiplying signed numbers. For example, $(+4) \times (+8) = +32$ and $(-4) \times (-8) = +32$. If the signs are opposite, the product is negative. For example, $(+4) \times (-8) = -32$ and $(-4) \times (+8) = -32$. When more than two factors are multiplied together, the sign of the product is determined by how many negative factors are present. If there are an odd number of negative factors then the product is negative, whereas an even number of negative factors indicates a positive product. For instance, $(+4) \times (-8) \times (-2) = +64$ and $(-4) \times (-8) \times (-2) = -64$.

The rules for dividing signed numbers are similar to multiplying signed numbers. If the dividend and divisor have the same sign, the quotient is positive. If the dividend and divisor have opposite signs, the quotient is negative. For example, $(-4) \div (+8) = -0.5$.

Below is a list of the field properties of number systems for quick reference.

- Subtraction:
  - $a - b = a + (-b)$
- Additive Identity:
  - $a + 0 = a$
  - $0 + a = a$
- Additive Inverse:
  - $a + (-a) = 0$
  - $(-a) + a = 0$
- Associative:
  - $(a + b) + c = a + (b + c)$ for addition
  - $(ab)c = a(bc)$ for multiplication
- Closure:
  - $a + b$ is a real number for addition
  - ab is a real number for multiplication
- Commutative:
  - $a + b = b + a$ for addition
  - $ab = ba$ for multiplication
- Distributive:
  - $a(b + c) = ab + ac$
  - $(a + b)c = ac + bc$

35

- Multiplicative Identity:
  - $a \cdot 1 = a$
  - $1 \cdot a = a$
- Multiplicative Inverse:
  - $a \cdot a^{-1} = 1$
  - $a^{-1} \cdot a = 1$
- Division:
  - $a \div b = \dfrac{a}{b} = a \cdot b^{-1} = a \cdot \dfrac{1}{b}$

WORKING WITH EXPONENTS

A positive integer exponent indicates the number of times the base is multiplied by itself. Anything raised to the zero power is equal to 1. A negative integer exponent means you must take the reciprocal of the result of the corresponding positive integer exponent. A fractional exponent signifies a root. The following formulas all apply to exponents:

$$x^0 = 1$$

$$x^{-n} = \frac{1}{x^n}$$

$$\left(\frac{a}{b}\right)^{-1} = \frac{b}{a}$$

$$(x^a)^b = x^{ab}$$

$$(xy)^n = x^n y^n$$

$$\left(\frac{x}{y}\right)^n = \frac{x^n}{y^n}$$

$$0^0 = \text{undefined}$$

A root, or *Square Root*, is a number that when multiplied by itself yields a real number. For example, $\sqrt{4} = +2, -2$ because $(-2) \times (-2) = 4$ and $(2) \times (2) = 4$. Further, $\sqrt{9} = +3, -3$ because $(-3) \times (-3) = 9$ and $(3) \times (3) = 9$. Therefore, +2 and -2 are square roots of 4 while +3 and -3 are square roots of 9.

Another important rule to understand with regard to exponents is called the *Order of Operations*.

1. Solve expressions inside any parentheses using the order below; then return to 2.
2. Solve any exponents.
3. Do all remaining multiplication and division in the order they appear from left to right.
4. Perform any addition and subtraction as it appears from left to right.

IMPORTANT CONCEPTS

Commonly in algebra and other upper-level fields of math you find yourself working with mathematical expressions that do not equal each other. The statement comparing such expressions with symbols such as < (less than) or > (greater than) is called an *Inequality*. An example of an inequality is $7x > 5$. To solve for x, simply divide both sides by 7 and the solution is shown to be $x > \frac{5}{7}$. Graphs of the solution set of inequalities are represented on a number line. Open circles are used to show that an expression approaches a number but is never quite equal to that number.

Conditional Inequalities are those with certain values for the variable that will make the condition true and other values for the variable where the condition will be false. *Absolute Inequalities* can have any real number as the value for the variable to make the condition true, while there is no real number value for the variable that will make the condition false.

Solving inequalities is done by following the same rules as for solving equations with the exception that when multiplying or dividing by a negative number the direction of the inequality sign must be flipped or reversed. *Double Inequalities* are situations where two inequality statements apply to the same variable expression. An example of this is $-c < ax + b < c$.

Two more comparisons used frequently in algebra are ratios and proportions. A *Ratio* is a comparison of two quantities, expressed in a number of different ways. Ratios can be listed as "a to b", "a:b", or "a/b". Examples of ratios are miles per hour (miles/hour), meters per second (meters/second), miles per gallon (miles/gallon), etc..

A statement of two equal ratios is a *Proportion*, such as $\frac{m}{b} = \frac{w}{z}$. If Fred travels 2 miles in 1 hour and Jane travels 4 miles in 2 hours, their speeds are said to be proportional because $\frac{2}{1} = \frac{4}{2}$. In a proportion, the product of the numerator of the first ratio and the denominator of the second ratio is equal to the product of the denominator of the first ratio and the numerator of the second ratio. Using the previous example we see that $m \times z = b \times w$, thus $2 \times 2 = 1 \times 4$.

A *Weighted Mean*, or weighted average, is a mean that uses "weighted" values. The formula is weighted mean $= \frac{w_1x_1 + w_2x_2 + w_3x_3 \ldots + w_nx_n}{w_1 + w_2 + w_3 + \cdots + w_n}$. Weighted values, such as $w_1, w_2, w_3, \ldots w_n$ are assigned to each member of the set $x_1, x_2, x_3, \ldots x_n$. If calculating weighted mean, make sure a weight value for each member of the set is used.

A fraction that contains a fraction in the numerator, denominator, or both is called a *Complex Fraction*. These can be solved in a number of ways; with the simplest being by following the order of operations as stated earlier. For example, $\frac{\left(\frac{4}{7}\right)}{\left(\frac{5}{8}\right)} = \frac{0.571}{0.625} = 0.914$. Another way to solve this problem is to multiply the fraction in the numerator by the reciprical of the fraction in the denominator. For example, $\frac{\left(\frac{4}{7}\right)}{\left(\frac{5}{8}\right)} = \frac{4}{7} \times \frac{8}{5} = \frac{32}{35} = 0.914$.

EQUATIONS AND GRAPHING

When algebraic functions and equations are shown graphically, they are usually shown on a *Cartesian Coordinate Plane*. The Cartesian coordinate plane consists of two number lines placed perpendicular to each other, and intersecting at the zero point, also known as the origin. The horizontal number line is known as the *x*-axis, with positive values to the right of the origin, and negative values to the left of the origin. The vertical number line is known as the *y*-axis, with positive values above the origin, and negative values below the origin. Any point on the plane can be identified by an ordered pair in the form (*x,y*), called coordinates. The *x*-value of the coordinate is called the abscissa, and the *y*-value of the coordinate is called the ordinate. The two number lines divide the plane into four quadrants: I, II, III, and IV.

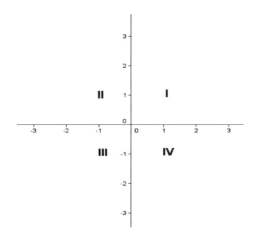

Before learning the different forms equations can be written in, it is important to understand some terminology. A ratio of the change in the vertical distance to the change in horizontal distance is called the *Slope*. On a graph with two points, (x_1, y_1) and (x_2, y_2), the slope is represented by the formula $= \frac{y_2 - y_1}{x_2 - x_1}$; $x_1 \neq x_2$. If the value of the slope is positive, the line slopes upward from left to right. If the value of the slope is negative, the line slopes downward from left to right. If the *y*-coordinates are the same for both points, the slope is 0 and the line is a *Horizontal Line*. If the *x*-coordinates are the same for both points, there is no slope and the line is a *Vertical Line*. Two or more lines that have equal slopes are *Parallel Lines*. *Perpendicular Lines* have slopes that are negative reciprocals of each other, such as $\frac{a}{b}$ and $\frac{-b}{a}$.

Equations are made up of monomials and polynomials. A *Monomial* is a single variable or product of constants and variables, such as x, $2x$, or $\frac{2}{x}$. There will never be addition or subtraction symbols in a monomial. Like monomials have like variables, but they may have different coefficients. *Polynomials* are algebraic expressions which use addition and subtraction to combine two or more monomials. Two terms make a binomial; three terms make a trinomial; etc. The *Degree of a Monomial* is the sum of the exponents of the variables. The *Degree of a Polynomial* is the highest degree of any individual term.

As mentioned previously, equations can be written many ways. Below is a list of the many forms equations can take.

- Standard Form: $Ax + By = C$; the slope is $\frac{-A}{B}$ and the y-intercept is $\frac{C}{B}$
- *Slope Intercept Form*: $y = mx + b$, where m is the slope and b is the *y*-intercept
- Point-Slope Form: $y - y_1 = m(x - x_1)$, where m is the slope and (x_1, y_1) is a point on the line
- Two-Point Form: $\frac{y - y_1}{x - x_1} = \frac{y_2 - y_1}{x_2 - x_1}$, where (x_1, y_1) and (x_2, y_2) are two points on the given line
- *Intercept Form*: $\frac{x}{x_1} + \frac{y}{y_1} = 1$, where $(x_1, 0)$ is the point at which a line intersects the *x*-axis, and $(0, y_1)$ is the point at which the same line intersects the *y*-axis

38

Equations can also be written as $ax + b = 0$, where $a \neq 0$. These are referred to as *One Variable Linear Equations*. A solution to an equation is called a *Root*. In the case where we have the equation $5x + 10 = 0$, if we solve for x we get a solution of $x = -2$. In other words, the root of the equation is -2. This is found by first subtracting 10 from both sides, which gives $5x = -10$. Next, simply divide both sides by the coefficient of the variable, in this case 5, to get $x = -2$. This can be checked by plugging -2 back into the original equation $(5)(-2) + 10 = -10 + 10 = 0$.

The *Solution Set* is the set of all solutions of an equation. In our example, the solution set would simply be -2. If there were more solutions (there usually are in multivariable equations) then they would also be included in the solution set. When an equation has no true solutions, this is referred to as an *Empty Set*. Equations with identical solution sets are *Equivalent Equations*. An *Identity* is a term whose value or determinant is equal to 1.

CALCULATIONS USING POINTS

Sometimes you need to perform calculations using only points on a graph as input data. Using points, you can determine what the midpoint and distance are. If you know the equation for a line you can calculate the distance between the line and the point.

To find the *Midpoint* of two points (x_1, y_1) and (x_2, y_2), average the x-coordinates to get the x-coordinate of the midpoint, and average the y-coordinates to get the y-coordinate of the midpoint. The formula is midpoint $= \left(\frac{x_1 + x_2}{2}, \frac{y_1 + y_2}{2} \right)$.

The *Distance* between two points is the same as the length of the hypotenuse of a right triangle with the two given points as endpoints, and the two sides of the right triangle parallel to the x-axis and y-axis, respectively. The length of the segment parallel to the x-axis is the difference between the x-coordinates of the two points. The length of the segment parallel to the y-axis is the difference between the y-coordinates of the two points. Use the Pythagorean Theorem $a^2 + b^2 = c^2$ or $c = \sqrt{a^2 + b^2}$ to find the distance. The formula is: distance $= \sqrt{(x_2 - x_1)^2 + (y_2 - y_1)^2}$.

When a line is in the format $Ax + By + C = 0$, where A, B, and C are coefficients, you can use a point (x_1, y_1) not on the line and apply the formula $d = \frac{|Ax_1 + By_1 + C|}{\sqrt{A^2 + B^2}}$ to find the distance between the line and the point (x_1, y_1).

> **Review Video: Distance & Midpoint for Points on the Coordinate Plane**
> Visit mometrix.com/academy and enter code: 973653

SYSTEMS OF EQUATIONS

Systems of Equations are a set of simultaneous equations that all use the same variables. A solution to a system of equations must be true for each equation in the system. *Consistent Systems* are those with at least one solution. *Inconsistent Systems* are systems of equations that have no solution. Systems of equations may be solved using one of four methods: substitution, addition, transformation of the augmented matrix and using the trace feature on a graphing calculator. The three most common methods are explained in the following passages.

To solve a system of linear equations by *substitution*, start with the easier equation and solve for one of the variables. Express this variable in terms of the other variable. Substitute this expression in the other equation, and solve for the other variable. The solution should be expressed in the form (x, y). Substitute the values into both of the original equations to check your answer. Consider the following problem.

Solve the system using substitution:

$$x + 6y = 15$$

$$3x - 12y = 18$$

$$x = 15 - 6y$$

$$3(15 - 6y) - 12y = 18$$

$$45 - 18y - 12y = 18$$

$$30y = 27$$

$$y = \frac{27}{30} = \frac{9}{10} = 0.9$$

$$x = 15 - 6(0.9) = 15 - 5.4 = 9.6$$

Now check both equations

$$9.6 + 6(0.9) = 9.6 + 5.4 = 15$$

$$3(9.6) - 12(0.9) = 28.8 - 10.8 = 18$$

Therefore, the solution is $(9.6, 0.9)$.

To solve a system of equations using *elimination* or *addition*, begin by rewriting both equations in standard form $Ax + By = C$. Check to see if the coefficients of one pair of like variables add to zero. If not, multiply one or both of the equations by a non-zero number to make one set of like variables add to zero. Add the two equations to solve for one of the variables. Substitute this value into one of the original equations to solve for the other variable. Check your work by substituting into the other equation. Next, we will solve the same problem as above, but using the addition method.

Solve the system using substitution:

$$x + 6y = 15$$

$$3x - 12y = 18$$

For practice we will multiply the first equation by 6 and the second equation by -2 to get rid of the x variables.

$$6x + 36y = 90$$

$$-6x + 24y = -36$$

Add the equations together to get $60y = 54$. Thus, $y = \frac{54}{60} = \frac{9}{10} = 0.9$.

Plug the value for y back in to either of the original equations to get the value for x.

$$x + 6(0.9) = 15$$

$$x = 15 - 5.4 = 9.6$$

Now check both equations

$$9.6 + 6(0.9) = 9.6 + 5.4 = 15$$

$$3(9.6) - 12(0.9) = 28.8 - 10.8 = 18$$

Therefore, the solution is (9.6, 0.9).

Using the *trace feature on a calculator* requires that you rewrite each equation, isolating the y-variable on one side of the equal sign. Enter both equations in the graphing calculator and plot the graphs simultaneously. Use the trace cursor to find where the two lines cross. Use the zoom feature if necessary, to obtain more accurate results. Always check your answer by substituting into the original equations. The trace method is likely to be less accurate than other methods due to the resolution of graphing calculators, but is a useful tool to provide an approximate answer.

> **Review Video: Substitution and Elimination for Solving Linear Systems**
> Visit mometrix.com/academy and enter code: 958611

POLYNOMIAL ALGEBRA

To multiply two binomials, follow the *FOIL* method. FOIL stands for:

- **F**irst: Multiply the first term of each binomial
- **O**uter: Multiply the outer terms of each binomial
- **I**nner: Multiply the inner terms of each binomial
- **L**ast: Multiply the last term of each binomial

Using FOIL $(Ax + By)(Cx + Dy) = ACx^2 + ADxy + BCxy + BDy^2$.

To divide polynomials, begin by arranging the terms of each polynomial in order of one variable. You may arrange in ascending or descending order, but be consistent with both polynomials. To get the first term of the quotient, divide the first term of the dividend by the first term of the divisor. Multiply the first term of the quotient by the entire divisor and subtract that product from the dividend. Repeat for the second and successive terms until you either get a remainder of zero or a remainder whose degree is less than the degree of the divisor. If the quotient has a remainder, write the answer as a mixed expression in the form: quotient $+ \frac{\text{remainder}}{\text{divisor}}$.

Rational Expressions are fractions with polynomials in both the numerator and the denominator; the value of the polynomial in the denominator cannot be equal to zero. To add or subtract rational expressions, first find the common denominator, then rewrite each fraction as an equivalent fraction with the common denominator. Finally, add or subtract the numerators to get the numerator of the answer, and keep the common denominator as the denominator of the answer. When multiplying rational expressions factor each polynomial and cancel like factors (a factor which appears in both the numerator and the denominator). Then, multiply all remaining factors in the numerator to get the numerator of the product, and multiply the remaining factors in the denominator to get the denominator of the product. Remember – cancel entire factors, not individual terms. To divide rational expressions, take the reciprocal of the divisor (the rational expression you are dividing by) and multiply by the dividend.

Below are patterns of some special products to remember: *perfect trinomial squares*, the *difference between two squares*, the *sum and difference of two cubes*, and *perfect cubes*.

- Perfect Trinomial Squares: $x^2 + 2xy + y^2 = (x + y)^2$ or $x^2 - 2xy + y^2 = (x - y)^2$
- Difference between Two Squares: $x^2 - y^2 = (x + y)(x - y)$
- Sum of Two Cubes: $x^3 + y^3 = (x + y)(x^2 - xy + y^2)$
- Note: the second factor is NOT the same as a perfect trinomial square, so do not try to factor it further.
- Difference between Two Cubes: $x^3 - y^3 = (x - y)(x^2 + xy + y^2)$
- Again, the second factor is NOT the same as a perfect trinomial square.
- Perfect Cubes: $x^3 + 3x^2y + 3xy^2 + y^3 = (x + y)^3$ and $x^3 - 3x^2y + 3xy^2 - y^3 = (x - y)^3$

In order to *factor* a polynomial, first check for a common monomial factor. When the greatest common monomial factor has been factored out, look for patterns of special products: differences of two squares, the sum or difference of two cubes for binomial factors, or perfect trinomial squares for trinomial factors. If the factor is a trinomial but not a perfect trinomial square, look for a factorable form, such as $x^2 + (a + b)x + ab = (x + a)(x + b)$ or $(ac)x^2 + (ad + bc)x + bd = (ax + b)(cx + d)$.

For factors with four terms, look for groups to factor. Once you have found the factors, write the original polynomial as the product of all the factors. Make sure all of the polynomial factors are prime. Monomial factors may be prime or composite. Check your work by multiplying the factors to make sure you get the original polynomial.

> ### Review Video: Polynomials
> Visit mometrix.com/academy and enter code: 305005

SOLVING QUADRATIC EQUATIONS

The *Quadratic Formula* is used to solve quadratic equations when other methods are more difficult. To use the quadratic formula to solve a quadratic equation, begin by rewriting the equation in standard form $ax^2 + bx + c = 0$, where a, b, and c are coefficients. Once you have identified the values of the coefficients, substitute those values into the quadratic formula $= \frac{-b \pm \sqrt{b^2 - 4ac}}{2a}$. Evaluate the equation and simplify the expression. Again, check each root by substituting into the original equation. In the quadratic formula, the portion of the formula under the radical ($b^2 - 4ac$) is called the *Discriminant*. If the discriminant is zero, there is only one root: zero. If the discriminant is positive, there are two different real roots. If the discriminant is negative, there are no real roots.

To solve a quadratic equation by *Factoring*, begin by rewriting the equation in standard form, if necessary. Factor the side with the variable then set each of the factors equal to zero and solve the resulting linear equations. Check your answers by substituting the roots you found into the original equation. If, when writing the equation in standard form, you have an equation in the form $x^2 + c = 0$ or $x^2 - c = 0$, set $x^2 = -c$ or $x^2 = c$ and take the square root of c. If $c = 0$, the only real root is zero. If c is positive, there are two real roots—the positive and negative square root values. If c is negative, there are no real roots because you cannot take the square root of a negative number.

To solve a quadratic equation by *Completing the Square*, rewrite the equation so that all terms containing the variable are on the left side of the equal sign, and all the constants are on the right side of the equal sign. Make sure the coefficient of the squared term is 1. If there is a coefficient with the squared term, divide each term on both sides of the equal side by that number. Next, work with the coefficient of the single-variable term. Square half of this coefficient, and add that value to both sides. Now you can factor the left side (the side containing the variable) as the square of a binomial. $x^2 + 2ax + a^2 = C \Rightarrow (x + a)^2 = C$, where x is the variable, and a and C are constants. Take the square root of both sides and solve for the variable. Substitute the value of the variable in the original problem to check your work.

In order to solve a *Radical Equation*, begin by isolating the radical term on one side of the equation, and move all other terms to the other side of the equation. Look at the index of the radicand. Remember, if no number is given, the index is 2, meaning square root. Raise both sides of the equation to the power equal to the index of the radical. Solve the resulting equation as you would a normal polynomial equation. When you have found the roots, you must check them in the original problem to eliminate extraneous roots.

Review Video: Using the Quadratic Formula
Visit mometrix.com/academy and enter code: 163102

Data Analysis, Probability, and Statistics

STATISTICS

Statistics is the branch of mathematics that deals with collecting, recording, interpreting, illustrating, and analyzing large amounts of data. The following terms are often used in the discussion of data and statistics:

- Data – the collective name for pieces of information (singular is datum).
- Quantitative data – measurements (such as length, mass, and speed) that provide information about quantities in numbers
- Qualitative data – information (such as colors, scents, tastes, and shapes) that cannot be measured using numbers
- Discrete data – information that can be expressed only by a specific value, such as whole or half numbers; For example, since people can be counted only in whole numbers, a population count would be discrete data.
- Continuous data – information (such as time and temperature) that can be expressed by any value within a given range
- Primary data – information that has been collected directly from a survey, investigation, or experiment, such as a questionnaire or the recording of daily temperatures; Primary data that has not yet been organized or analyzed is called raw data.
- Secondary data – information that has been collected, sorted, and processed by the researcher
- Ordinal data – information that can be placed in numerical order, such as age or weight
- Nominal data – information that cannot be placed in numerical order, such as names or places

MEASURES OF CENTRAL TENDENCY

The quantities of mean, median, and mode are all referred to as measures of central tendency. They can each give a picture of what the whole set of data looks like with just a single number. Knowing what each of these values represents is vital to making use of the information they provide.

The mean, also known as the arithmetic mean or average, of a data set is calculated by summing all of the values in the set and dividing that sum by the number of values. For example, if a data set has 6 numbers and the sum of those 6 numbers is 30, the mean is calculated as 30/6 = 5.

The median is the middle value of a data set. The median can be found by putting the data set in numerical order, and locating the middle value. In the data set (1, 2, 3, 4, 5), the median is 3. If there is an even number of values in the set, the median is calculated by taking the average of the two middle values. In the data set, (1, 2, 3, 4, 5, 6), the median would be (3 + 4)/2 = 3.5.

The mode is the value that appears most frequently in the data set. In the data set (1, 2, 3, 4, 5, 5, 5), the mode would be 5 since the value 5 appears three times. If multiple values appear the same number of times, there are multiple values for the mode. If the data set were (1, 2, 2, 3, 4, 4, 5, 5), the modes would be 2, 4, and 5. If no value appears more than any other value in the data set, then there is no mode.

MEASURES OF DISPERSION

The standard deviation expresses how spread out the values of a distribution are from the mean. Standard deviation is given in the same units as the original data and is represented by a lower case sigma (σ).

A high standard deviation means that the values are very spread out. A low standard deviation means that the values are close together.

If every value in a distribution is increased or decreased by the same amount, the mean, median, and mode are increased or decreased by that amount, but the standard deviation stays the same.

If every value in a distribution is multiplied or divided by the same number, the mean, median, mode, and standard deviation will all be multiplied or divided by that number.

The range of a distribution is the difference between the highest and lowest values in the distribution. For example, in the data set (1, 3, 5, 7, 9, 11), the highest and lowest values are 11 and 1, respectively. The range then would be calculated as $11 - 1 = 10$.

The three quartiles are the three values that divide a data set into four equal parts. Quartiles are generally only calculated for data sets with a large number of values. As a simple example, for the data set consisting of the numbers 1 through 99, the first quartile (Q1) would be 25, the second quartile (Q2), always equal to the median, would be 50, and the third quartile (Q3) would be 75. The difference between Q1 and Q3 is known as the interquartile range.

PROBABILITY

Probability is a branch of statistics that deals with the likelihood of something taking place. One classic example is a coin toss. There are only two possible results: heads or tails. The likelihood, or probability, that the coin will land as heads is 1 out of 2 (1/2, 0.5, 50%). Tails has the same probability. Another common example is a 6-sided die roll. There are six possible results from rolling a single die, each with an equal chance of happening, so the probability of any given number coming up is 1 out of 6.

Review Video: Intro to Probability
Visit mometrix.com/academy and enter code: 212374

Terms frequently used in probability:

- Event – a situation that produces results of some sort (a coin toss)
- Compound event – event that involves two or more items (rolling a pair of dice; taking the sum)
- Outcome – a possible result in an experiment or event (heads, tails)
- Desired outcome (or success) – an outcome that meets a particular set of criteria (a roll of 1 or 2 if we are looking for numbers less than 3)
- Independent events – two or more events whose outcomes do not affect one another (two coins tossed at the same time)
- Dependent events – two or more events whose outcomes affect one another (two cards drawn consecutively from the same deck)
- Certain outcome – probability of outcome is 100% or 1
- Impossible outcome – probability of outcome is 0% or 0
- Mutually exclusive outcomes – two or more outcomes whose criteria cannot all be satisfied in a single outcome (a coin coming up heads and tails on the same toss)

Theoretical probability is the likelihood of a certain outcome occurring for a given event. It can be determined without actually performing the event. It is calculated as P (probability of success) = (desired outcomes)/(total outcomes).

45

Example:

There are 20 marbles in a bag and 5 are red. The theoretical probability of randomly selecting a red marble is 5 out of 20, (5/20 = 1/4, 0.25, or 25%).

Most of the time, when we talk about probability, we mean theoretical probability. Experimental probability, or relative frequency, is the number of times an outcome occurs in a particular experiment or a certain number of observed events.

While theoretical probability is based on what *should* happen, experimental probability is based on what *has* happened. Experimental probability is calculated in the same way as theoretical, except that actual outcomes are used instead of possible outcomes.

Theoretical and experimental probability do not always line up with one another. Theoretical probability says that out of 20 coin tosses, 10 should be heads. However, if we were actually to toss 20 coins, we might record just 5 heads. This doesn't mean that our theoretical probability is incorrect; it just means that this particular experiment had results that were different from what was predicted.

> **Review Video: Theoretical and Experimental Probability**
> Visit mometrix.com/academy and enter code: 444349

When trying to calculate the probability of an event using the (desired outcomes)/(total outcomes formula), you may frequently find that there are too many outcomes to individually count them. Permutation and combination formulas offer a shortcut to counting outcomes. The primary distinction between permutations and combinations is that permutations take into account order, while combinations do not. To calculate the number of possible groupings, there are two necessary parameters: the number of items available for selection and the number to be selected. The number of permutations of r items given a set of n items can be calculated as $_nP_r = \frac{n!}{(n-r)!}$. The number of combinations of r items given a set of n items can be calculated as $_nC_r = \frac{n!}{r!(n-r)!}$ or $_nC_r = \frac{_nP_r}{r!}$.

Example:

Suppose you want to calculate how many different 5-card hands can be drawn from a deck of 52 cards. This is a combination since the order of the cards in a hand does not matter. There are 52 cards available, and 5 to be selected. Thus, the number of different hands is $_{52}C_5 = \frac{52!}{5! \times 47!} = 2,598,960$.

COMMON CHARTS AND GRAPHS

A bar graph is a graph that uses bars to compare data, as if each bar were a ruler being used to measure the data. The graph includes a scale that identifies the units being measured.

A line graph is a graph that connects points to show how data increases or decreases over time. The time line is the horizontal axis. The connecting lines between data points on the graph are a way to more clearly show how the data changes.

A pictograph is a graph that uses pictures or symbols to show data. The pictograph will have a key to identify what each symbol represents. Generally, each symbol stands for one or more objects.

A pie chart or circle graph is a diagram used to compare parts of a whole. The full pie represents the whole, and it is divided into sectors that each represent something that is a part of the whole. Each sector or slice of the pie is either labeled to indicate what it represents, or explained on a key associated with the chart. The size of each slice is determined by the percentage of the whole that the associated quantity represents. Numerically, the angle measurement of each sector can be computed by solving the proportion: $x/360 = $ part/whole.

A histogram is a special type of bar graph where the data are grouped in intervals (for example 20-29, 30-39, 40-49, etc.). The frequency, or number of times a value occurs in each interval, is indicated by the height of the bar. The intervals do not have to be the same amount but usually are (all data in ranges of 10 or all in ranges of 5, for example). The smaller the intervals, the more detailed the information.

A stem-and-leaf plot is a way to organize data visually so that the information is easy to understand. A stem-and-leaf plot is simple to construct because a simple line separates the stem (the part of the plot listing the tens digit, if displaying two-digit data) from the leaf (the part that shows the ones digit). Thus, the number 45 would appear as 4 | 5. The stem-and-leaf plot for test scores of a group of 11 students might look like the following:

```
9 | 5
8 | 1, 3, 8
7 | 0, 2, 4, 6, 7
6 | 2, 8
```

A stem-and-leaf plot is similar to a histogram or other frequency plot, but with a stem-and-leaf plot, all the original data is preserved. In this example, it can be seen at a glance that nearly half the students scored in the 70's, yet all the data has been maintained. These plots can be used for larger numbers as well, but they tend to work better for small sets of data as they can become unwieldy with larger sets.

Measurement and Geometry

ANGLES

An angle is formed when two lines or line segments meet at a common point. It may be a common starting point for a pair of segments or rays, or it may be the intersection of lines. Angles are represented by the symbol ∠.

The vertex is the point at which two segments or rays meet to form an angle. If the angle is formed by intersecting rays, lines, and/or line segments, the vertex is the point at which four angles are formed. The pairs of angles opposite one another are called vertical angles, and their measures are equal.

An acute angle is an angle with a degree measure less than 90°.

A right angle is an angle with a degree measure of exactly 90°.

An obtuse angle is an angle with a degree measure greater than 90° but less than 180°.

A straight angle is an angle with a degree measure of exactly 180°. This is also a semicircle.

A reflex angle is an angle with a degree measure greater than 180° but less than 360°.

A full angle is an angle with a degree measure of exactly 360°.

> **Review Video: <u>Angles</u>**
> Visit mometrix.com/academy and enter code: 264624

Two angles whose sum is exactly 90° are said to be complementary. The two angles may or may not be adjacent. In a right triangle, the two acute angles are complementary.

Two angles whose sum is exactly 180° are said to be supplementary. The two angles may or may not be adjacent. Two intersecting lines always form two pairs of supplementary angles. Adjacent supplementary angles will always form a straight line.

Two angles that have the same vertex and share a side are said to be adjacent. Vertical angles are not adjacent because they share a vertex but no common side.

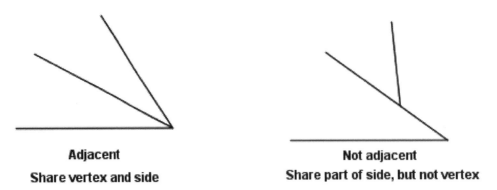

Adjacent
Share vertex and side

Not adjacent
Share part of side, but not vertex

When two parallel lines are cut by a transversal, the angles that are between the two parallel lines are interior angles. In the diagram below, angles 3, 4, 5, and 6 are interior angles.

When two parallel lines are cut by a transversal, the angles that are outside the parallel lines are exterior angles. In the diagram below, angles 1, 2, 7, and 8 are exterior angles.

When two parallel lines are cut by a transversal, the angles that are in the same position relative to the transversal and a parallel line are corresponding angles. The diagram below has four pairs of corresponding angles: angles 1 and 5; angles 2 and 6; angles 3 and 7; and angles 4 and 8. Corresponding angles formed by parallel lines are congruent.

When two parallel lines are cut by a transversal, the two interior angles that are on opposite sides of the transversal are called alternate interior angles. In the diagram below, there are two pairs of alternate interior angles: angles 3 and 6, and angles 4 and 5. Alternate interior angles formed by parallel lines are congruent.

When two parallel lines are cut by a transversal, the two exterior angles that are on opposite sides of the transversal are called alternate exterior angles. In the diagram below, there are two pairs of alternate exterior angles: angles 1 and 8, and angles 2 and 7. Alternate exterior angles formed by parallel lines are congruent.

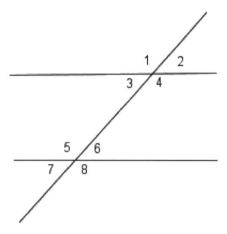

When two lines intersect, four angles are formed. The non-adjacent angles at this vertex are called vertical angles. Vertical angles are congruent. In the diagram, $\angle ABD \cong \angle CBE$ and $\angle ABC \cong \angle DBE$.

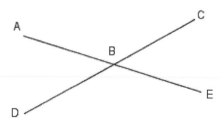

TRIANGLES

An equilateral triangle is a triangle with three congruent sides. An equilateral triangle will also have three congruent angles, each 60°. All equilateral triangles are also acute triangles.

An isosceles triangle is a triangle with two congruent sides. An isosceles triangle will also have two congruent angles opposite the two congruent sides.

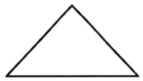

A scalene triangle is a triangle with no congruent sides. A scalene triangle will also have three angles of different measures. The angle with the largest measure is opposite the longest side, and the angle with the smallest measure is opposite the shortest side.

An acute triangle is a triangle whose three angles are all less than 90°. If two of the angles are equal, the acute triangle is also an isosceles triangle. If the three angles are all equal, the acute triangle is also an equilateral triangle.

A right triangle is a triangle with exactly one angle equal to 90°. All right triangles follow the Pythagorean Theorem. A right triangle can never be acute or obtuse.

An obtuse triangle is a triangle with exactly one angle greater than 90°. The other two angles may or may not be equal. If the two remaining angles are equal, the obtuse triangle is also an isosceles triangle.

PYTHAGOREAN THEOREM

The side of a triangle opposite the right angle is called the hypotenuse. The other two sides are called the legs. The Pythagorean Theorem states a relationship among the legs and hypotenuse of a right triangle: $a^2 + b^2 = c^2$, where a and b are the lengths of the legs of a right triangle, and c is the length of the hypotenuse. Note that this formula will only work with right triangles.

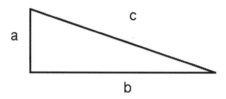

GENERAL RULES

The Triangle Inequality Theorem states that the sum of the measures of any two sides of a triangle is always greater than the measure of the third side. If the sum of the measures of two sides were equal to the third side, a triangle would be impossible because the two sides would lie flat across the third side and there would be no vertex. If the sum of the measures of two of the sides was less than the third side, a closed figure would be impossible because the two shortest sides would never meet.

The sum of the measures of the interior angles of a triangle is always 180°. Therefore, a triangle can never have more than one angle greater than or equal to 90°.

In any triangle, the angles opposite congruent sides are congruent, and the sides opposite congruent angles are congruent. The largest angle is always opposite the longest side, and the smallest angle is always opposite the shortest side.

The line segment that joins the midpoints of any two sides of a triangle is always parallel to the third side and exactly half the length of the third side.

SIMILARITY AND CONGRUENCE RULES

Similar triangles are triangles whose corresponding angles are equal and whose corresponding sides are proportional. Represented by AA. Similar triangles whose corresponding sides are congruent are also congruent triangles.

Three sides of one triangle are congruent to the three corresponding sides of the second triangle. Represented as SSS.

Two sides and the included angle (the angle formed by those two sides) of one triangle are congruent to the corresponding two sides and included angle of the second triangle. Represented by SAS.

Two angles and the included side (the side that joins the two angles) of one triangle are congruent to the corresponding two angles and included side of the second triangle. Represented by ASA.

Two angles and a non-included side of one triangle are congruent to the corresponding two angles and non-included side of the second triangle. Represented by AAS.

Note that AAA is not a form for congruent triangles. This would say that the three angles are congruent, but says nothing about the sides. This meets the requirements for similar triangles, but not congruent triangles.

51

AREA AND PERIMETER FORMULAS

The perimeter of any triangle is found by summing the three side lengths; $P = a + b + c$. For an equilateral triangle, this is the same as $P = 3s$, where s is any side length, since all three sides are the same length.

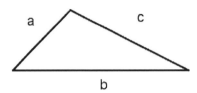

The area of any triangle can be found by taking half the product of one side length (base or b) and the perpendicular distance from that side to the opposite vertex (height or h). In equation form, $A = \frac{1}{2}bh$. For many triangles, it may be difficult to calculate h, so using one of the other formulas given here may be easier.

Review Video: <u>Area and Perimeter of a Triangle</u>
Visit mometrix.com/academy and enter code: 853779

Another formula that works for any triangle is $A = \sqrt{s(s-a)(s-b)(s-c)}$, where A is the area, s is the semiperimeter $s = \frac{a+b+c}{2}$, and a, b, and c are the lengths of the three sides.

The area of an equilateral triangle can be found by the formula $A = \frac{\sqrt{3}}{4}s^2$, where A is the area and s is the length of a side. You could use the $30° - 60° - 90°$ ratios to find the height of the triangle and then use the standard triangle area formula, but this is faster.

The area of an isosceles triangle can be found by the formula, $A = \frac{1}{2}b\sqrt{a^2 - \frac{b^2}{4}}$, where A is the area, b is the base (the unique side), and a is the length of one of the two congruent sides. If you do not remember this formula, you can use the Pythagorean Theorem to find the height so you can use the standard formula for the area of a triangle.

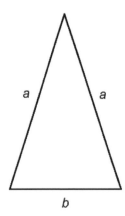

POLYGONS

Congruent figures are geometric figures that have the same size and shape. All corresponding angles are equal, and all corresponding sides are equal. It is indicated by the symbol ≅.

Congruent polygons

Similar figures are geometric figures that have the same shape, but do not necessarily have the same size. All corresponding angles are equal, and all corresponding sides are proportional, but they do not have to be equal. It is indicated by the symbol ∼.

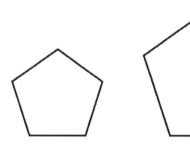

Similar polygons

Note that all congruent figures are also similar, but not all similar figures are congruent.

Line of Symmetry: The line that divides a figure or object into two symmetric parts. Each symmetric half is congruent to the other. An object may have no lines of symmetry, one line of symmetry, or more than one line of symmetry.

Lines of symmetry:

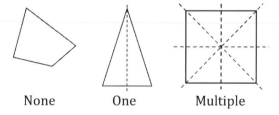

None   One   Multiple

Quadrilateral: A closed two-dimensional geometric figure composed of exactly four straight sides. The sum of the interior angles of any quadrilateral is 360°.

Parallelogram: A quadrilateral that has exactly two pairs of opposite parallel sides. The sides that are parallel are also congruent. The opposite interior angles are always congruent, and the

53

consecutive interior angles are supplementary. The diagonals of a parallelogram bisect each other. Each diagonal divides the parallelogram into two congruent triangles.

Trapezoid: Traditionally, a quadrilateral that has exactly one pair of parallel sides. Some math texts define trapezoid as a quadrilateral that has at least one pair of parallel sides. Because there are no rules governing the second pair of sides, there are no rules that apply to the properties of the diagonals of a trapezoid.

Rectangles, rhombuses, and squares are all special forms of parallelograms.

Rectangle: A parallelogram with four right angles. All rectangles are parallelograms, but not all parallelograms are rectangles. The diagonals of a rectangle are congruent.

Rhombus: A parallelogram with four congruent sides. All rhombuses are parallelograms, but not all parallelograms are rhombuses. The diagonals of a rhombus are perpendicular to each other.

Square: A parallelogram with four right angles and four congruent sides. All squares are also parallelograms, rhombuses, and rectangles. The diagonals of a square are congruent and perpendicular to each other.

A quadrilateral whose diagonals bisect each other is a parallelogram. A quadrilateral whose opposite sides are parallel (2 pairs of parallel sides) is a parallelogram.

A quadrilateral whose diagonals are perpendicular bisectors of each other is a rhombus. A quadrilateral whose opposite sides (both pairs) are parallel and congruent is a rhombus.

A parallelogram that has a right angle is a rectangle. (Consecutive angles of a parallelogram are supplementary. Therefore, if there is one right angle in a parallelogram, there are four right angles in that parallelogram.)

A rhombus with one right angle is a square. Because the rhombus is a special form of a parallelogram, the rules about the angles of a parallelogram also apply to the rhombus.

AREA AND PERIMETER FORMULAS

The area of a square is found by using the formula $A = s^2$, where and s is the length of one side.

The perimeter of a square is found by using the formula $P = 4s$, where s is the length of one side. Because all four sides are equal in a square, it is faster to multiply the length of one side by 4 than to add the same number four times. You could use the formulas for rectangles and get the same answer.

> **Review Video: <u>Area and Perimeter of a Square</u>**
> Visit mometrix.com/academy and enter code: 620902

The area of a rectangle is found by the formula $A = lw$, where A is the area of the rectangle, l is the length (usually considered to be the longer side) and w is the width (usually considered to be the shorter side). The numbers for l and w are interchangeable.

The perimeter of a rectangle is found by the formula $P = 2l + 2w$ or $P = 2(l + w)$, where l is the length, and w is the width. It may be easier to add the length and width first and then double the result, as in the second formula.

> **Review Video: <u>Area and Perimeter of a Rectangle</u>**
> Visit mometrix.com/academy and enter code: 933707

The area of a parallelogram is found by the formula $A = bh$, where b is the length of the base, and h is the height. Note that the base and height correspond to the length and width in a rectangle, so this formula would apply to rectangles as well. Do not confuse the height of a parallelogram with the length of the second side. The two are only the same measure in the case of a rectangle.

The perimeter of a parallelogram is found by the formula $P = 2a + 2b$ or $P = 2(a + b)$, where a and b are the lengths of the two sides.

Review Video: Area and Perimeter of a Parallelogram
Visit mometrix.com/academy and enter code: 718313

The area of a trapezoid is found by the formula $A = \frac{1}{2}h(b_1 + b_2)$, where h is the height (segment joining and perpendicular to the parallel bases), and b_1 and b_2 are the two parallel sides (bases). Do not use one of the other two sides as the height unless that side is also perpendicular to the parallel bases.

The perimeter of a trapezoid is found by the formula $P = a + b_1 + c + b_2$, where a, b_1, c, and b_2 are the four sides of the trapezoid.

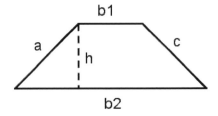

Review Video: Area and Perimeter of a Trapezoid
Visit mometrix.com/academy and enter code: 587523

CIRCLES

The center is the single point inside the circle that is equidistant from every point on the circle. (Point O in the diagram below.)

The radius is a line segment that joins the center of the circle and any one point on the circle. All radii of a circle are equal. (Segments OX, OY, and OZ in the diagram below.)

The diameter is a line segment that passes through the center of the circle and has both endpoints on the circle. The length of the diameter is exactly twice the length of the radius. (Segment XZ in the diagram below.)

The area of a circle is found by the formula $A = \pi r^2$, where r is the length of the radius. If the diameter of the circle is given, remember to divide it in half to get the length of the radius before proceeding.

The circumference of a circle is found by the formula $C = 2\pi r$, where r is the radius. Again, remember to convert the diameter if you are given that measure rather than the radius.

Concentric circles are circles that have the same center, but not the same length of radii. A bulls-eye target is an example of concentric circles.

An arc is a portion of a circle. Specifically, an arc is the set of points between and including two points on a circle. An arc does not contain any points inside the circle. When a segment is drawn from the endpoints of an arc to the center of the circle, a sector is formed.

A central angle is an angle whose vertex is the center of a circle and whose legs intercept an arc of the circle. Angle XOY in the diagram above is a central angle. A minor arc is an arc that has a measure less than 180°. The measure of a central angle is equal to the measure of the minor arc it intercepts. A major arc is an arc having a measure of at least 180°. The measure of the major arc can be found by subtracting the measure of the central angle from 360°.

A semicircle is an arc whose endpoints are the endpoints of the diameter of a circle. A semicircle is exactly half of a circle.

An inscribed angle is an angle whose vertex lies on a circle and whose legs contain chords of that circle. The portion of the circle intercepted by the legs of the angle is called the intercepted arc. The measure of the intercepted arc is exactly twice the measure of the inscribed angle. In the diagram below, angle ABC is an inscribed angle. $\overset{\frown}{AC} = 2(m\angle ABC)$.

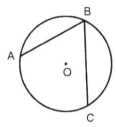

Any angle inscribed in a semicircle is a right angle. The intercepted arc is 180°, making the inscribed angle half that, or 90°. In the diagram below, angle ABC is inscribed in semicircle ABC, making angle ABC equal to 90°.

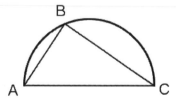

A chord is a line segment that has both endpoints on a circle. In the diagram below, $\overline{EB}$ is a chord.

Secant: A line that passes through a circle and contains a chord of that circle. In the diagram below, $\overleftrightarrow{EB}$ is a secant and contains chord $\overline{EB}$.

A tangent is a line in the same plane as a circle that touches the circle in exactly one point. While a line segment can be tangent to a circle as part of a line that is tangent, it is improper to say a tangent can be simply a line segment that touches the circle in exactly one point. In the diagram below, $\overleftrightarrow{CD}$ is tangent to circle A. Notice that $\overline{FB}$ is not tangent to the circle. $\overline{FB}$ is a line segment that touches the circle in exactly one point, but if the segment were extended, it would touch the circle in a second point.

The point at which a tangent touches a circle is called the point of tangency. In the diagram below, point B is the point of tangency.

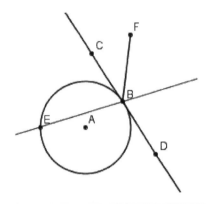

Review Video: <u>Tangent Lines of a Circle</u>
Visit mometrix.com/academy and enter code: 780167

Analytical Writing Test

The Analytical Writing portion of the GRE consists of two 30-minute writing sections: one covering an Issue Analysis topic, and one covering an Argument Analysis topic.

The Analytical Writing Test may be the section of the GRE for which candidates are least prepared. There are a number of reasons why this may be so. For one thing, many students have a general dislike of writing, which they associate with hard labor. Given the choice between composing an essay and answering a series of multiple-choice questions, most students will choose the latter. Still, the predominant reason why students arrive at the testing center unprepared for the Analytical Writing section of the exam is that they simply do not know how to prepare. On the Verbal and Quantitative Reasoning sections, studying is straightforward: simply learn the different questions types, and the content to be covered. This process may not always be easy, but at least it is fairly obvious. For many college students, however, preparing to sit down and write a couple of extended essays can be daunting. Moreover, students, whose undergraduate coursework did not require a great deal of writing, may not have performed such a task since taking a freshman composition course. Therefore, the basic structure of a persuasive or analytical essay may be long forgotten, and students may be discouraged, feeling that it is impossible to learn to write in a short period of time.

This despair is unnecessary. Even though a crash course in Analytical Writing may not turn you into a best-selling author, it can teach you the fundamentals of composition, so that you can achieve an excellent score on the GRE. Preparing for the Analytical Writing section does not need to be any more difficult than preparing for the other sections of the GRE. In fact, it is not much different. To get you ready to excel on the Analytical Writing section, we will take a close look at the two types of essays required, and discuss ways to approach each of them. Then, we will create a basic plan for composing your responses, so that, when you enter the testing facility, you will have already completed most of the hard work.

Analytical Writing responses are graded according to a simple protocol: Each essay is examined by two readers, who score it on a scale of zero to six. If the two scores are within one point of each other, then they are averaged and finalized. However, if the difference between the scores is greater than one point, then a third reader is called in to arbitrate. Your final score on the Analytical Writing Test will be the average of your scores on the Issue and Argument Analysis essays.

The Analytical Writing response scoring system is "holistic", which means that it is based on a general view of the responses, rather than on any specific or individual criteria. This means that minor and occasional spelling and grammar mistakes will not have an effect on your grade. The scoring criteria for the two essays are basically the same. A top score of six will be awarded to essays that are consistently convincing, well articulated, and clear. Essays that achieve these qualities only sometimes or most of the time will earn a 4 or 5. Essays that demonstrate flashes of competence, but more often fail to show competency, are given a 3. Essays that are marked by serious flaws in reasoning and poor writing will be a given a 2. Finally, a 1 will only be given to responses that either make no sense, or are not on-topic.

Now, for some good news: all of the possible prompts that are used on the GRE are listed on the ETS website. You should spend at least a few hours looking over all of these prompts, taking a position, and imagining a few basic arguments. Look up any words that you do not already know. There are probably too many potential prompts for it to be practical to examine each one in depth, but you can at least familiarize yourself with the question format, and the kinds of topics that are likely to appear on the exam. Also, acquainting yourself with the essay prompts will stimulate your brain to start thinking along those lines in the weeks running up to the exam. You may see a newspaper or magazine article that pertains to one of the potential prompts, or you may just find yourself mulling over one of these issues. By giving your brain a chance to digest these potential topics, you will improve your chances of producing a thoughtful, well-rounded essay. At the very least, when you finally sit down to take the GRE, you should have no excuse for being surprised.

Issue Analysis

For the Issue Analysis essay, you will be presented with a topic, and will have to write out your views on that topic within the 30 minutes allowed. There is not a "correct" answer to the problem. Rather, you must choose a position on the issue, organize your ideas, and develop them into a cohesive and coherent stance. You will be scored on how well you are able to utilize standard written English, organize and explain your ideas, and support those ideas with reasons and examples.

BRAINSTORM

Spend the first three to five minutes brainstorming ideas. Write down any ideas that you might have on the issue, regardless of which side it supports. The purpose of this is to extract any relevant information from the recesses of your memory. Put the ideas that support one side of the argument into one grouping, and then, further down on the page, group the ideas that support the other side. You can use either scratch paper or the word processor to quickly jot down your thoughts and ideas. Using the word processor is highly recommended, though, particularly if you are a fast typist.

STRENGTH THROUGH DIVERSITY

The best papers will contain a diversity of examples and reasoning. As you brainstorm, consider different perspectives. Not only are there two sides to every issue, but also there are also countless perspectives that can be considered. On any issue, different groups are impacted, with many reaching the same conclusion or position, but through vastly different paths. Try to "see" the issue through as many different eyes as you can. Look at it from every angle, and from every vantage point. The more diverse the reasoning used, the more balanced the paper will become, and the better the score.

For example, the issue of free trade is not just two-sided, it impacts politicians, domestic (US) manufacturers, foreign manufacturers, the US economy, the world economy, strategic alliances, retailers, wholesalers, consumers, unions, workers, and the exchange of more than just goods, but also of ideas, beliefs, and cultures. The more of these angles that you can approach the issue from, the more solid your reasoning will be, and the stronger your position will be. Furthermore, do not just use information regarding how the issue impacts other people: draw liberally from your own experience, and your own observations. Explain a personal experience that you have had, and your own emotional experience from that moment. Anything that you have seen in your community, or observed in society, can be expanded upon to further round out your position on the issue.

PICK A SIDE

Once you have finished with your creative flow, stop and review it. Which side were you able to come up with more supporting information? It is easy to be biased, and to have a side that you believe in and support with your own personal opinion. While enthusiasm for a viewpoint is important, the ability to have a thorough and comprehensive coverage of an issue, and the position that you choose, is much more important. This is not about your personal convictions. Each idea that you can write about and expand upon is a defensive tool. Therefore, pick a side on the issue to defend based upon what you have the most defensive tools to work with. In fact, you may find that this coincides nicely with what you do believe, since you probably know more information that supports what you believe, than information that detracts from what you believe.

WEED THE GARDEN

Every garden of ideas gets weeds in it. The ideas that you brainstormed over are going to be random pieces of information of mixed value. Go through it methodically, and pick out the ones that are the best. The best ideas are strong arguments that it will be easy to write a few sentences or a paragraph about.

CREATE A LOGICAL FLOW

You will then take these notes and begin to shape them into a rough outline. The outline is your map for writing the essay: it reminds you of where you are trying to go, as well as where you will need to make stops along the way. Too often, students will assume that they have a firm grasp over the topic, and will just begin writing without creating a basic outline. Then, they get distracted by something in the testing center, or become overly focused on one aspect of their argument, and end up forgetting to include an important part of their response. By composing an outline, you can save yourself the trouble of keeping your entire argument in your head as you write.

The structure of your outline, and hence your essay, should be the same no matter what topic or position you are discussing. In the first paragraph, you will lay out the issue to be discussed, and indicate your position. In the second, third, and fourth paragraphs, you will give reasons and examples in support of your position. Finally, in the fifth paragraph, you will summarize and generalize your position. There is nothing profound or mysterious about this format: it is the essay structure that has been drilled into your head since middle school. Also, do not worry about lack of originality: GRE readers spend five minutes at the most on each essay, and they – frankly – do not have time to appreciate essays that use unconventional organization. Instead, they look for essays that are easy to read (even if a little dull!), and that are original in their content, rather than their structure. Besides, your job becomes much easier when you have a simple template to use, no matter what topic you are discussing.

START YOUR ENGINES

You now have a logical flow of main ideas with which to begin writing. Start by expanding on the issues in the sequence that you have set out for yourself. Pace yourself, and do not spend too much time on any one of the ideas that you are expanding upon: you want to have time for all of them. So, make sure that you watch your time. If you have thirty minutes left to write out your ideas, and you have ten ideas, then you can only use three minutes per idea. It can be a daunting task to cram a lot of information down in words, within a short amount of time. However, if you pace yourself, you can get through it all. And, if you find that you are falling behind, speed up. Move through each idea more quickly, and spend less time expanding upon the ideas in order to catch back up.

Once you finish expanding upon each idea, go back to your brainstorming session up above, where you typed out your ideas. Go ahead and delete the ideas as you write about them. This will let you see what you need to write about next, and also allow you to pace yourself and see what you have left to cover.

PARAGRAPH DETAILS

As mentioned above, in the first paragraph, you need to begin by articulating the topic under consideration. In other words, outline the basic issue first, without declaring your own position. You do not want to simply duplicate the language that was used in the prompt. For instance, consider the example topic: *"Laws should exist solely to keep people from hurting one another; there should not be laws to prevent people from hurting themselves."* An effective way to introduce the issue might be, *"There is a longstanding debate over whether or not laws should extend to the private behavior of citizens."* Note how this sentence, bland though it may be, outlines the issue at hand, without indicating which side you will be taking. It is important for you to be able to express the topic in an impartial manner, so that the reader can become oriented with the discussion. If you simply launch into an impassioned argument, the reader may feel alienated or confused.

After the basic outline of the topic issue, your first paragraph needs to include a summary of your own position. This summary must be clear and concise: there should be no confusion over where you stand after this first paragraph. Continuing with our example, after introducing the topic, the author might write, *"It is my belief that since individual behavior, no matter how private, will inevitably affect other people, laws should be extended to prevent self-inflicted damage to individuals and their property."* After such a statement, there is no doubt where the author stands: he or she is in favor of legislation forbidding individuals from harming themselves. Also, note the use of the personal pronouns, as in *"It is my belief"*. On the Issue Analysis essay, you should feel free to claim your opinions (after all, the essay is all about presenting your perspective). This is preferable to ambiguous expressions like *"one believes"*. The whole point of this first paragraph is to show that you know what you are talking about, and to show exactly where you stand on the issue.

Once your position has been clearly articulated, you can move on to supporting it in the subsequent paragraphs. This is when your list of brainstormed ideas will come in handy. Pare the list down to the best three to five ideas or examples, and then rank them from best to worst. You always want to open with your strongest point. In our example, the author's strongest point is probably that self-destructive behavior is actually damaging to other people as well. The author will want to make this argument in the second paragraph. When you are establishing the reasons for your position, try to be as specific as possible. This does not mean that you need to worry about providing direct quotes or exact numbers, but you should be able to cite specific instances and trends that support your case.

Also, as you begin to expand your argument in the supporting paragraphs, keep in mind your list of potential counterarguments. The GRE reader will want you to acknowledge and rebut any obvious arguments that run counter to your own position. If you ignore clear contradictions, the reader will penalize you. For instance, the author of our example essay would need to admit that some people argue that drug abuse, failure to wear a seatbelt, and even suicide are private decisions that only affect the individuals involved. The author might argue that these people ignore the toll that such self-destructive behavior takes on the economy, the community, and the world as a whole. The author might give a couple of quick examples to show how seemingly individual behavior affects other people. By describing the ways in which this counterargument is unreasonable, the author will strengthen his own position.

In all of the following support paragraphs, the guidelines are the same. Try to be as specific as possible, and be sure to address any legitimate counterarguments to your position. Make sure that all of your examples make sense, and have a clear application to the problem being discussed. If you are going to use examples from your personal life, make sure that you can focus on the parts that are relevant to your argument, rather than getting bogged down in setting an elaborate scene.

As a general rule, if a story or anecdote is going to take more than three sentences to deliver, it is probably not worth the trouble. You want your supporting paragraphs to be brimming with ideas and evidence, not meandering or digressive.

As you are making your argument in the supporting paragraphs, do not be afraid to use clichéd transitional phrases like "*next*", "*another*", and "*finally*". Advanced composition classes will try to move students beyond such obvious structural markers, but on the GRE you can feel free to dust off some of these hackneyed expressions in the interest of clarity. As we have already discussed, the readers of your essay will not be hoping for unorthodox structure: they want a solid essay with good ideas, and an easy-to-read format. There is one exception: it is perhaps too formulaic to begin each of your supporting paragraphs with "*first*", "*second*", etc. Other than that, go ahead and make your transitions obvious, so that the reader will spend his or her time focusing on the strength of your argument, rather than the subtlety of your style.

After you have given three or four specific detailed arguments or examples in support of your position, it is time to wrap up your essay in a conclusion paragraph. Here, again, it is fitting to announce your finale with a phrase like "*in conclusion*" or "*as you can see*". (Of course, if you use the latter expression, you had better be confident that your argument was clear.) Then, give a one-sentence recapitulation of your argument. Too often, students take up the entire conclusion paragraph by giving a complete review of the essay up to that point. This is unnecessary: provided that you have been clear, so far, your reader is only going to be bored by an abridged version of what he or she has already read.

Instead, you should use the conclusion paragraph to first summarize, and then generalize your argument. In other words, expand the scope of your argument to take notice of any larger issues or themes. Returning to our hypothetical essay, the author might use the conclusion paragraph to assert that, since private self-destructive behavior really does affect other people, individuals should try to be more conscious of the ways in which they mistreat themselves. Note that this kind of generalization can be overdone: it would probably be a bit much, for instance, for the author to declare that his argument proves that all living creatures are one. The GRE readers do not want you to use your conclusion paragraphs to advance your vision of the cosmos, but rather to show an awareness of the ways in which your topic connects with other issues. If you can suggest some ways that your argument resonates beyond the parameters of your essay, then that will be enough.

DO NOT PANIC

Panicking will not put down any more words on paper for you, and it is not helpful. When you first see the topic, if your mind goes as blank as the page on which you have to type out your paper, take a deep breath. Force yourself to mechanically go through the steps listed above. Ask yourself, who would be impacted by this issue? Would you be impacted? Would someone you know be impacted? Who stands to benefit or lose from this issue?

Secondly, do not get clock fever. It is easy to get overwhelmed when you are looking at a page that does not seem to have much text, there is a lot of blank space further down, your mind is full of random thoughts and feeling confused, and the clock is ticking down faster than you would like. However, you brainstormed first, so that you do not have to keep coming up with ideas. If you are running out of time, and you have a lot of ideas that you have not expanded upon, then do not be afraid to make some cuts. Start picking the best ideas that you have left, and expand on those few. Do not feel like you have to write down all of your ideas.

CHECK YOUR WORK

It is more important to have a shorter paper that is well written and well organized, than a longer paper that is poorly written and poorly organized. Do not keep writing about a subject just to add words and sentences, and certainly do not start repeating yourself. Expand on the ideas that you identified in the brainstorming session, and make sure that you save yourself a few minutes at the end to go back and check your work.

Leave time at the end, at least three minutes, to go back and check over your work. Reread and make sure that everything you have written makes sense and flows. Clean up any spelling or grammar mistakes that you might have made. If you see anything that needs to be moved around, such as a paragraph that would fit in better somewhere else, cut and paste it into that new location. Also, go ahead and delete any brainstorming ideas that you were unable to expand upon, and clean up any other extraneous information, which you might have typed, that does not fit into your paper.

As you proofread, make sure that there are not any fragments or run-ons. Check for sentences that are too short or too long. If a sentence is too short, look to see if you have an identifiable subject and verb. If it is too long, then break it up into two separate sentences. Watch out for any "big" words that you may have used. It is okay to use difficult vocabulary words, but be positive that you are using them correctly. While the position that you are defending is important, it needs to be solid and convincing; not fancy. You are not trying to impress anyone with your vocabulary; you are trying to impress them with your ability to develop and express ideas.

SHORTCUT KEYS

Spend some time on your keyboard getting familiar with the shortcut keys to cut, copy, and paste. It will help you to quickly move text around on your paper. First, highlight the text that you wish to move or copy, and then press the following keys:

To Copy = Ctrl+C

To Cut = Ctrl+X

To Paste = Ctrl+V

You must hold down the Ctrl key, and then tap the "C", "X", or "V" key to perform the desired function.

Argument Analysis

For the Argument Analysis essay, you will be presented with an argument, and you must write out a critique on it within the 30 minutes allowed. There is not a "correct" side to the argument, and you are not being asked about your own personal views on the topic. You must evaluate the argument, organize your ideas, and develop them into a cohesive and coherent critique.

You will be scored on how well you are able to utilize standard written English, organize and explain your ideas, and support those ideas with reasons and examples.

BREAKDOWN

From the very beginning, your focus should be on the argument introduced in the prompt. The prompt will be longer than the one for the Issue Analysis essay, so take your time, and read it carefully. It is typical for the prompt to be written from a particular viewpoint. For instance, a prompt might begin by saying that the following statement appeared on the editorial page of a newspaper, in a report published by a certain institution, or in a newsletter distributed by a specific political organization. Pay attention to the source of the argument, as this will help you to begin your analysis. You want to be sensitive to any prejudices that might be natural to a particular author. As you read the argument that follows, bear the source in mind, and see if that generates any insights.

Spend the first three to five minutes breaking the argument down into little pieces by asking yourself a series of questions: What assumptions does the argument make? What explanations does it rely upon? What authority does it stand upon? What supports the reasoning used? What evidence is used? What examples are provided?

Then, ask some follow-up questions: What changes to the argument would make it stronger? What changes to the argument would make it weaker? What would help you to reach a stronger conclusion? What would make it more logical? What would make it more balanced?

FINDINGS

Let us look at an example. The following argument was taken from a guide for would-be musicians:

Fledgling musicians need to establish themselves with small record labels before seeking attention from more well-known entities. However, the rise of the internet and do-it-yourself production have made it easier than ever for novice musicians to create a quality product on a small budget. There is also a much larger market these days for musicians to make and sell their music without any assistance from a label. Some musicians enjoy the process of developing and marketing their songs, while others would rather leave the work to their representatives. The most important thing is to have a good time while you are making music.

Remember that you are not being asked about your personal beliefs or convictions. You are being asked whether the argument is well reasoned. Based on the questions that you have asked yourself, you should have a good understanding as to how irrefutable the logic of the argument is. Make a decision as to how strong or weak the argument is.

To begin with, let us examine the basic parts of an argument: the premise, assumptions, reasoning, and conclusion. Before you create your outline for the Argument Analysis essay, you will need to identify these elements within the prompt. The premise of an argument is its starting point: the agreed-upon beginning of its reasoning. In the example, the premise of the argument is that beginning musicians should first establish themselves with a small label. The author has not yet told us why this is necessary, or what the benefit of it will be. We are simply supposed to assume the premise to be true as we continue with the argument. Of course, in many cases, you will find that the premise of an argument is nonsensical or unsupported. Note that you are not required to agree with the premise of an argument. At this point, it is enough just to identify it, and then move on to an examination of the other components of the argument.

The assumptions of the argument are perhaps the most difficult elements to identify, since they are not made explicitly. The assumptions are those things that the author must take for granted as being true in order to make his or her point. They are all of the unstated bridges between premise and conclusion. As a critical reader, it is your job to articulate the underlying assumptions, and decide whether they make sense. In the example argument, the author makes a number of assumptions:

1. All musicians want to be on a major label.
2. All kinds of music can be created on a low budget.
3. There is a larger market for all kinds of music.

You could probably find more assumptions implicit in the argument, but three good assumptions will suffice. It is clear that there are some major problems with these assumptions. Specifically, it seems that the author is often guilty of generalizing his beliefs. This is not necessarily a problem, since every author must generalize a bit in order to discuss abstract ideas. However, do the assumptions made by this author undermine his or her cause?

Before we go on to consider the reasoning of an argument, let us review some of the most common kinds of faulty assumptions that are found on the GRE. In the previous paragraph, we saw some good examples of generalization assumptions, in which the author makes blanket statements about an entire category. Often, we will find that exceptions to the author's assumptions cast the entire argument into doubt. Another common kind of assumption is the causal assumption, in which the author suggests that there is only one cause for a given effect, and that the removal of the cause will therefore cause an immediate removal of the effect. For instance, an author might suggest that, because smoking causes lung cancer, the prohibition of tobacco would bring an end to the disease. Of course, there are other causes of lung cancer besides tobacco, so this is a faulty causal assumption.

The arguments on the GRE may also contain faulty sampling assumptions, in which the author makes a sweeping statement based on a very small amount of data. One of the most common kinds of sampling assumptions is when the author universalizes his or her own personal experience. For instance, *"None of my friends have been harassed on the subway, so to say there is a growing menace there is incorrect."* In this case, the author erroneously assumes that the experience of his or her friends is a fair representation of the entire subway-riding population. Sampling assumptions may also be faulty when the author uses a particular survey or study to prove something other than what the survey set out to prove.

The final kind of assumption that you should be wary of is the analogy assumption. An author will sometimes suggest that two things are comparable when, in fact, they are not. Typically, the author will point out a characteristic of one of the things, and then suggest that it must be true of the other as well. Of course, if the things in question are not really analogous, then this assumption must be false. For example, consider the following statement: *"Cats do not enjoy the heat; after all, dogs try to avoid direct sunlight, and both of these animals are common house pets."* The author makes a statement about dogs, and then asks you to assume it to be true of cats, since these are domestic animals as well. Regardless of whether or not you agree that dogs try to avoid direct sunlight, it is clearly absurd to suggest that dogs and cats are exactly the same just because they are both kept as pets. This is an example of a faulty analogy assumption.

After you identify the author's premise and assumptions, you should quickly note his or her conclusion. The conclusion should be the general point that is supported by all of the author's reasoning. It is usually indicated by words like "therefore", "thus", "as a result", and "hence". The conclusion of the argument is almost always the last sentence. Occasionally, though, the GRE will try to confuse you by adding on an irrelevant final sentence. Indeed, the final sentence in our example prompt somewhat fits this description. Up to that point, the author discusses how best to establish oneself in the music industry, and then, in the final sentence, he declares that the most important thing in music is to enjoy yourself. This sentence sounds like a conclusion ("*The most important thing...*"), but it clearly has no relation to the rest of the prompt.

Finally, before you create your outline and write your essay, you need to consider the reasoning of the argument. The reasoning of an argument is the specific set of ideas and examples that the author uses to move from premise to conclusion. The best kind of reasoning is clear, precise, and relevant to the subject. If the author endeavors to support his or her argument with examples, they must be appropriate. There are a number of ways in which reasoning can be defective. Sometimes, the author will dilute a good argument by including irrelevant information. Other times, an author will have good reasoning, but will draw an incorrect conclusion from it. Occasionally, the reasoning might also contain gaps that require impossible assumptions by the reader.

In the case of our example prompt, there are several problems with the author's reasoning. First, the author begins by declaring that novice musicians should start with a small record label. He then goes on to undermine this suggestion by asserting that musicians now have the capability to make quality music on their own. Well, one might wonder, which is it? Seek out a small label, or do it yourself? The author continues by stating that independent musicians have a much larger market for their products than ever before. This would seem to support the notion of working without a record label. Again, the author subsequently weakens this idea by declaring that some musicians would prefer to leave the business and production work to someone else. Finally, as we have already mentioned, the author concludes with a sentence that is basically irrelevant.

ORGANIZE

In the first paragraph, you should articulate your general analysis of the argument, making sure to identify the premise and conclusion. In the succeeding two or three paragraphs, you should discuss the specific strengths and weaknesses of the argument's reasoning and assumptions. And, in the final paragraph, you should summarize your analysis, and describe some ways in which the argument could be improved.

FIRST PARAGRAPH

To begin with, you will need to establish the general form of the argument, and indicate the results of your analysis. Using our example prompt, an effective essay might begin by stating the general premise: new musicians should start out with a small record label. It might go on to say that the reasoning of the argument only partially supports this premise, and, indeed, just as often supports an entirely different premise; namely that musicians can be successful, independent of any record label. Finally, it might state that the "conclusion" statement of the argument is irrelevant to the preceding argument. There is no need to go into too much depth with your introductory paragraph: simply assert your general judgment of the argument. If someone were to read only this paragraph, then they should be able to get an "executive summary" of the entire paper.

BODY PARAGRAPH

In your supporting paragraphs, you can expand your critique. As with the Issue Analysis essay, it is always advisable to lead with your most powerful ideas. (The only exception to this strategy is that you probably do not want to begin by discussing the conclusion of the argument.) For some arguments, the most important issue may be faulty assumptions. In others, the most outstanding errors may be in the reasoning. For the example prompt, the greatest weakness seems to be that the author argues in favor of two different ideas. In other words, the primary fault of the argument is one of reasoning. The author does make some problematic assumptions, but these are not as worrisome as the ineffective reasoning and nonsensical conclusion. An effective critique of this argument would begin by attacking the poor reasoning and conclusion, and would only discuss the faulty assumptions if time allowed.

CONCLUSION PARAGRAPH

In the conclusion paragraph of your Argument Analysis essay, summarize your analysis, and – more importantly – recommend some ways to improve the argument. These suggestions should be clear, specific, and restricted to the parameters of the discussion. In other words, do not suggest that the argument needs to be changed in a radical way. Remember that this essay is not meant to be a forum for your opinions. Limit your suggestions to the specific reasoning and assumptions that are used by the author, without distorting the premise or conclusions from the author's basic intent. For instance, a critique of the example prompt might end by suggesting that the author decide which method for success he wants to endorse, and then eliminate all of the information that diverges from this thesis. Furthermore, the critique might recommend that the author abandon his conclusion sentence in favor of a recapitulation of the streamlined thesis. In any case, you do not want to spend the concluding paragraph of this essay ruminating on the implications of the argument, as you would on the Issue Analysis essay. Restrict your remarks to the argument as it is written, and you will be rewarded.

FINAL REVIEW

Let us take a moment to consider a few issues of style. First of all, you should try to make your spelling as perfect as possible, without becoming obsessive. The GRE does not dock your score for misspellings, but readers will admit that serial errors can be distracting and off-putting. The word processor program that is used on the GRE does not include a spell-check function, so students, who are used to relying on the computer to correct spelling errors, will have to be more diligent. If you suspect that you may be spelling a certain word wrong, then see if you can use a synonym instead. If you absolutely have to use the questionable word, then do your best and move on. Remember that, unless your spelling errors are rampant, you will not be penalized.

A similar hang-up for many students on the Analytical Writing Test is the question of vocabulary. In general, you want to use as many specific and vivid words as possible, without overwriting. For instance, avoid describing something as "very good" when you could say that it was "fantastic", and do not say "dog" when you really mean "schnauzer". The GRE readers are trained to pay more attention to your reasoning than to your diction, but they will nevertheless reward those students who write energetically and colorfully. There are some limits, however. You should never use a sophisticated word unless you are absolutely sure of the definition, and unless it can be used in a natural way. The GRE readers are extremely sensitive to pretentiousness, and they will be quick to punish you for showing off. If you feel like you are going out of your way just to use a particular word, it is probably not worth it. Also, never use any slang or inappropriate language. This may seem obvious, but every year some students are penalized for using vulgar or overly-familiar language on the GRE. The Analytical Writing section of the GRE is one time when it is good to be bland with your writing: you do not want to run the risk of offending your reader.

For this reason, be very careful about how you use personal anecdotes in the Issue Analysis essay. When used properly, illustrative stories are an excellent way to add life to your argument. However, there is a danger of straying too far from the task at hand, so only use these anecdotes when you can do so quickly and appropriately. Also, never use personal anecdotes on the Argument Analysis essay: this essay is meant to be strictly a critique of the prompt argument.

If you can only remember one piece of advice regarding the Analytical Writing section, it is this: depth rather than breadth. That is, concentrate on a few great ideas, and explicate them fully, rather than trying to dazzle the reader with every single relevant thought that flies into your brain. In the end, your score will be much higher if you make your points clear, precise, and detailed.

Finally, a word about preparation: After you have studied the basic essay outlines described above, the best way to prepare for the Analytical Writing section of the GRE is to set up a timer and practice composition. Remember to use the list of possible prompts that is posted on the ETS website. It is very important to time yourself so that you can develop a feeling for how long you should take reading, planning, and writing your responses. For most students, it is typical for the Issue Analysis essay to run between 400 and 750 words, and for the Argument Analysis essay to run between 300 and 650 words. However, do not worry about achieving any specific length. Concentrate, instead, on making each essay as strong as possible. After you have practiced each of the essays a few times, you will be amazed at how easy it has become!

Final Note

Depending on your test-taking preferences and personality, the Analytical Writing test will probably be your hardest or your easiest test. You are required to go through the entire process of writing a paper in 30 minutes or less, which can be quite a challenge.

Focus upon each of the steps listed above. Go through the process of creative flow first, generating ideas and thoughts about the topic. Then, organize those ideas into a smooth logical flow. Pick out the ones that are best from the list you have created. Decide upon which side of the issue you will discuss, or your overall impression of the argument.

Create a recognizable structure in your paper, with an introductory paragraph explaining what you have decided upon, and what your main points will be. Use the body paragraphs to expand on those main points, and have a conclusion that wraps up the issue or argument.

Save a few moments to go back and review what you have written. Clean up any minor mistakes that you might have had, and give it those last few critical touches that can make a huge difference. Finally, be proud and confident of what you have written, and prepare yourself for the next phase of the exam.

GRE Practice Test

Section 1

Analytical Writing

Time – 30 minutes

ANALYZE AN ISSUE

You will have a choice between two Issue topics. Each topic will appear as a brief quotation that states or implies an issue of general interest. Read each topic carefully; then decide on which topic you could write a more effective and well-reasoned response. You will have 45 minutes to plan and compose a response that presents your perspective on the topic you select. A response on any other topic will receive a zero. You are free to accept, reject, or qualify the claim made in the topic you selected, as long as the ideas you present are clearly relevant to the topic. Support your views with reasons and examples drawn from such areas as your reading, experience, observations, or academic studies.

GRE readers, who are college and university faculty, will read your response and evaluate its overall quality, based on how well you do the following:

- consider the complexities and implications of the issue
- organize, develop, and express your ideas on the issue
- support your ideas with relevant reasons and examples
- control the elements of standard written English

You may want to take a few minutes to think about the issue and to plan a response before you begin writing. Because the space for writing your response is limited, use the next page to plan your response. Be sure to develop your ideas fully and organize them coherently, but leave time to reread what you have written and make any revisions that you think are necessary.

Present your perspective on one of the issues below, using relevant reasons and/or examples to support your views.

Topic No: 1

> "All government, indeed every human benefit and enjoyment, every virtue, and every prudent act, is founded on compromise and barter."

Topic No: 2

> "Democracy is when the indigent, and not the men of property, are the rulers."

Write the topic number of the issue you choose on the line at the top right corner of the answer booklet labeled "Analytical Writing 1: Issue."

Section 2

Analytical Writing

Time – 30 minutes

ANALYZE AN ARGUMENT

You will have 30 minutes to plan and write a critique of an argument presented in the form of a short passage. A critique of any other argument will receive a score of zero. Analyze the line of reasoning in the argument. Be sure to consider what, if any, questionable assumptions underlie the thinking and, if evidence is cited, how well it supports the conclusion. You can also discuss what sort of evidence would strengthen or refute the argument, what changes in the argument would make it more logically sound, and what additional information might help you better evaluate its conclusion. *Note that you are NOT being asked to present your views on the subject.*

GRE readers, who are college and university faculty, will read your critique and evaluate its overall quality, based on how well you

- identify and analyze important features of the argument
- organize, develop, and express your critique of the argument
- support your critique with relevant reasons and examples
- control the elements of standard written English

Before you begin writing, you may want to take a few minutes to evaluate the argument and plan a response. Because the space for writing your response is limited, use the next page to plan your response. Be sure to develop your ideas fully and organize them coherently, but leave time to reread what you have written and make any revisions that you think are necessary.

Discuss how well reasoned you find this argument.

Last year the city of East Lake decided to reallocate limited police resources by no longer responding to burglar alarms in commercial buildings. Since that change took effect, the number of break-ins in commercial buildings in East Lake has increased by 10 percent. In neighboring West Lake, the police continued to respond to burglar alarms in commercial buildings. There, the number of break-ins in commercial buildings declined in the last year by five percent. Therefore, if citizens want to reduce commercial break-ins in the region, they should pressure the East Lake Police Chief and local officials to restore the practice of police response to burglar alarms in commercial buildings.

Section 3

Verbal Reasoning

Time – 35 Minutes

25 Questions

Directions - Questions 1-7: For each blank select one entry from the corresponding column of choices. Fill all blanks in the way that best completes the text.

1. He believed that in order to (i) _____ the problem fully, he would need to understand all of its (ii) _____.

Blank (i)	Blank (ii)
a. solve	d. thoughts
b. address	e. nuances
c. comprehend	f. intricacies

2. The author's novel was (i) _____ but she managed to develop numerous (ii) _____ fully and enjoyably by its end.

Blank (i)	Blank (ii)
a. brief	d. plots
b. uninsightful	e. characters
c. long-winded	f. chapters

3. The rumors were (i) _____ and she welcomed the opportunity to (ii) _____ them.

Blank (i)	Blank (ii)
a. fabricated	d. refute
b. pertinent	e. enjoy
c. appealing	f. demystify

4. I was sorry to see her in that (i) _____, she looked so (ii) _____.

Blank (i)	Blank (ii)
a. situation	d. despondent
b. condition	e. arbitrary
c. mood	f. pensive

5. The disarray was _____; the office had to be closed for the day so all the furniture could be placed where it belonged, papers could be re-filed and a general cleaning done.

a. inconsequential
b. contemptible
c. severe
d. intermittent
e. trifling

72

6. He told the kids not to be so (i) _____ when he was gone. He was afraid they would (ii) _____ the babysitter.

Blank (i)
a. truculent
b. boisterous
c. egotistical

Blank (ii)
d. appease
e. endear
f. overwhelm

7. It was an _____ house with its vaulted ceilings, obviously expensive furniture and extravagant art covering the walls.

a. off-kilter
b. obstreperous
c. odious
d. obscure
e. ostentatious

8. Although (i) _____ by the young Prince Hal in Shakespeare's two *Henry IV* plays, the jovial character Falstaff fails to put away his youthful antics alongside the (ii)_____ prince and faces the consequences: in *Henry V*, the newly crowned king is forced to (iii) _____ his former friend.

Blank (i)
a. preferred
b. cherished
c. disgusted

Blank (ii)
d. maturing
e. impatient
f. tiresome

Blank (iii)
g. reform
h. renounce
i. restore

9. Tradition always has dictated that the (i) _____ King Richard III was responsible for the murder of his nephews, King Edward V, and Prince Richard, Duke of York. In her book *The Daughter of Time*, however, writer Josephine Tey (ii) _____ an alternative. She claimed instead that the real murderer was King Richard III's successor King Henry VII, and that the new king essentially rewrote history in his favor and (iii) _____ pinned the crime on his predecessor.

Blank (i)
a. popularly malevolent
b. utterly detestable
c. consistently suspicious

Blank (ii)
d. demanded
e. propounded
f. enlightened

Blank (iii)
g. eagerly
h. intentionally
i. retrospectively

Directions – Questions 10-17: Each passage in this group is followed by questions based on its content. After reading a passage, choose the best answer to each question. Answer all the questions following a passage on the basis of what is stated or <u>implied</u> in that passage.

Questions 10 to 12 are based on this passage.

It might be surprising to discover that Europe's first republic pre-dated the turn of the 11th century, long before Europe would see the rise of another such system. Around 870 AD, settlers from Norway began arriving in Iceland, and they eventually established a government system that gave all free men on the island a voice in legislative and judicial affairs. In approximately 930 AD, the leaders of Iceland created the Althing, considered the oldest parliament in the world. This system, and Iceland's identity as a republic, remained in place until 1262, when the decision of the Althing agreed to the Old Covenant and placed Iceland under the authority of the king of Norway. Iceland would not become a self-governing republic again until 1944, when the people of Iceland voted to end their political relationship with the kingdom of Denmark.

10. The passage indicates which of the following about the development of republics in Europe?

    a. Monarchy was a far more common system of government for most of Europe's history.
    b. The republic in Iceland ultimately was unable to withstand subjugation by another nation.
    c. It would be many years before another republic would develop in Europe.
    d. The republic that developed in Iceland lacked the stability it needed to survive.
    e. The modern republics in Europe have far more sophistication than Iceland's early republic.

Consider each of the three choices separately, and select all that apply.

11. The author of the passage fails to explain which of the following pieces of information that would complete the material within the passage?

    a. When Iceland converted to Christianity and thus infused Christian ideas into their political system.
    b. Why the first settlers to Iceland left Norway to seek out a new home.
    c. When Iceland came to be part of the kingdom of Denmark.

Consider each of the three choices separately, and select all that apply.

12. The mention of the Althing in relation to the Old Covenant suggests which of the following?

    a. There was a later covenant that followed the Old Covenant.
    b. The free men of Iceland had a voice in deciding on the Old Covenant.
    c. The people of Iceland resisted the union with Norway but ultimately agreed to it.

Questions 13 and 14 are based on this passage.

Iceland's Althing represented an important development in making the people of a nation an active part of the system that governed them. The meeting of the Althing brought together the main leaders of communities across the island; these local leaders all gathered to discuss and determine legal issues. The Althing also welcomed the free men of Iceland to present their claims, disputes, and the like. Althing attendees met at Lögberg, meaning "Law Rock," and the Lögsögumaður, or Lawspeaker, would oversee the event. The first activity was for the Lawspeaker to read a list of all applicable laws. The Lawspeaker would also offer necessary moderation in the case of disputes and provide an overriding sense of order. Also part of the Althing was the Lögretta, a legislative organization that supported the Lawspeaker by determining laws and settling legal disagreements.

13. The passage provides information about the Lawspeaker and his role at the Althing. Using the information in the passage as a guide, which of the following modern political roles is most similar to that of the Icelandic Lawspeaker?

    a. President
    b. Secretary of State
    c. President of the Senate
    d. Speaker of the House
    e. Lieutenant Governor

14. Based on the information provided in the passage, which of the following best summarizes the purpose of the Althing within Iceland's political system?

    a. To determine the laws of Iceland and to provide the free men with a role in their government.
    b. To provide a stable system of government for the free men of Iceland.
    c. To develop leaders within the communities and to make them as self-governing as possible.
    d. To unite the citizenry of Iceland against the invasion of foreign powers.
    e. To develop an island-wide legislative system that was consistent in application.

Questions 15 to 17 are based on this passage.

> Food science authorities have, in recent years, begun recommending that those persons who prepare their own whole grains begin by soaking the grains. Most grains contain phytic acid, which can prevent proper mineral absorption. For instance, phytic acid can block the body's ability to absorb iron from foods and thus raise the potential over time for anemia. Soaking the grains for several hours, however, reduces the level of phytic acid within them and makes the grains–such as rice, wheat, and quinoa–easier to digest. In fact, persons who struggle with digesting gluten, a common ingredient within grains like wheat, find that they are considerably more tolerant once the phytic acid has been reduced or removed. The soaking process is as simple as adding warm water to the grains for as long as twelve hours in advance of preparing them and then allowing the grains to sit in the water for a while.

15. Which of the following best describes the problem with phytic acid in grains?

    a. Phytic acid binds with the naturally occurring minerals in food and creates toxicity during cooking.
    b. Phytic acid is a natural ingredient within most foods, but it increases in whole grains and makes them difficult to digest.
    c. Phytic acid has a tendency to attach itself to gluten and thus make grains indigestible for persons with a gluten intolerance.
    d. Phytic acid attacks the body's digestive system and raises the potential for health problems.
    e. Phytic acid prevents the body from absorbing essential minerals that occur naturally in food.

Consider each of the three choices separately, and select all that apply.

16. The author of the passage indicates that soaking grains provides which of the following benefits?

    a. Soaking grains reduces the amount of phytic acid within them.
    b. Soaking grains removes the gluten and makes the grains digestible.
    c. Soaking grains improves the body's ability to digest them.

Select only one answer choice.

17. Based on the information provided within the passage, which of the following statements best defines the term food science?

a. The science of food preparation and the way that the chemical content of food alters during cooking.
b. The study of the chemical ingredients within food and the properties of those chemical ingredients.
c. The complex chemical ingredients that are found within grains and the way these chemicals affect the body.
d. The study of domestic food preparation and the differences between cooking food at home and the commercial preparation of food.
e. An emerging field that utilizes modern technology to study ancient grains and how the body utilizes them.

Questions 18 and 19 are based on this passage.

> The mystery of the Roanoke Colony never has been solved to any satisfaction, although a number of theories have arisen over the years. Some historians have suggested that the Roanoke colonists simply attempted to return to England but died in the effort. Cannibalism by area tribes and attacks by the Spanish have also been proposed as explanations for the disappearance of the colonists, but neither theory holds much weight among historical experts who argue conflicting evidence. Two other theories, however, remain popular as potential solutions. One historian has put forth the idea that the Roanoke colonists relocated away from the original settlement and eventually were killed by the powerful Chief Powhatan; the chief is said to have claimed responsibility for their deaths, because the colonists allied themselves with a tribe that did not support the powerful chief. Alternatively, other historians have located evidence to suggest that the people of Roanoke took shelter with area tribes and eventually became part of them. A number of Native American groups along the Mid-Atlantic claim European descent and share common features generally recognized as European.

18. Considering the information in the passage, which of the following could explain why historical experts reject the theory of the Spanish attacking Roanoke Colony?

a. Archeologists have not located any evidence of ammunition in the area around Roanoke Colony and have concluded that no guns were fired at the colonists.
b. Historical documents indicate that at the time the Roanoke colonists disappeared, the Spanish government had not yet discovered where the English had settled in the New World.
c. The English settlements in the New World had continued to anger the Spanish government, and led to ongoing tension between the two nations.
d. There is historical evidence that the Spanish government was working closely with Chief Powhatan to develop a treaty with the English.
e. The large number of Native American tribes around Roanoke Colony makes it more likely that cannibals attacked the settlers before the Spanish could.

76

19. Which of the following statements best summarizes the main point of the passage?

a. Most likely the colonists of Roanoke ultimately joined a friendly tribe in the area and intermarried with them, thereby producing offspring that carried European features.

b. Due to the lack of solid evidence regarding the events of Roanoke Colony, historians are in complete disagreement about why the Roanoke colonists disappeared.

c. The best explanation for what happened to the Roanoke colonists is most likely a combination of available theories, with some of them being killed and some of them joining other tribes.

d. There is a range of theories about what happened to the settlers at Roanoke Colony, but not enough evidence exists to explain the colony's disappearance with any certainty.

e. Historical evidence that survives indicates that the settlers at Roanoke Colony were caught in the metaphorical crossfire of warring Native American tribes and died as a result.

Directions – Questions 20-23: Select the *two* answer choices that, when used to complete the sentence, fit the meaning of the sentence as a whole *and* produce completed sentences that are alike in meaning.

20. Because the student had failed to take the prerequisite literature course, he found himself completely unable to determine the _____ within the poetry.

a. counterfeit
b. nuance
c. resonance
d. presumption
e. subtlety
f. pariah

21. To manage their growing debt and live within a budget, the couple decided to cut back and reduce any spending that was _____ to the support of basic needs.

a. superfluous
b. indispensable
c. unequivocal
d. indifferent
e. paramount
f. irrelevant

22. Although vehicle manufacturer had advertised that the car featured _____ storage space in the trunk, the new owners quickly discovered that very little actually fit there.

a. ostentatious
b. inadvertent
c. capacious
d. commodious
e. palatable
f. analogous

23 Having upheld her for years as the _____ of beauty, he was shocked to discover how much she had changed when he saw her at the high school reunion.

    a. conjecture
    b. exemplar
    c. precedent
    d. archetype
    e. malefactor
    f. dilettante

Directions – Questions 24-25: Each passage in this group is followed by questions based on its content. After reading a passage, choose the best answer to each question. Answer all the questions following a passage on the basis of what is stated or <u>implied</u> in that passage.

Questions 24 and 25 are based on this passage.

> If the Great Schism between East and West was not enough, the Western church experienced its own schism between 1378 and 1417. Unlike the earlier schism, though, this Western Schism resulted from political disputes among the factions within the church. Prior to the divide, the pope had moved from Rome to Avignon, France, during a period of crisis. Pope Gregory IX relocated to Rome in 1376, but he died soon thereafter. The Roman people demanded a Roman pope, but no qualified candidates could be found. As a result, the choice fell on a man from Naples, who ultimately became Pope Urban VI. He proved to be a disaster, and the now-sorry cardinals left Rome for Avignon again. There they elected the rival Pope Clement VII. Now the cardinals had elected two separate popes, and Rome and Avignon spent nearly three decades warring with each other, and the nations across Europe took sides as well. Order returned with the election of Pope Martin V in 1417, although Avignon continued a feeble resistance until 1429.

Consider each of the three choices separately, and select all that apply.

24. Based on the information in the passage, which of the following best distinguishes the cause of the Western Schism from the cause of the Great Schism?

    a. Social and political upheaval leading to a lack of continuity in church decisions.
    b. Internal conflict and political disagreements among the leaders of the church.
    c. Inability of church leadership to make astute decisions about appointees to the role of pope.

Select only one answer choice.

25. Which of the following statements best explains the implication in the final sentence of the passage?

a. Pope Martin V provided the stability that was needed for the pope to regain authority in Europe.

b. Although historians claim that the Western Schism ended in 1417, they fail to acknowledge the disputes that continued in Avignon until 1429.

c. Pope Martin V's appointment was approved by all factions, because the new pope had links both to Rome and to Avignon.

d. The confusion over papal appointments threw Europe into a state of confusion and led to other political disputes among nations.

e. The appointment of Pope Martin V was widely accepted, but a claimant to the papacy continued in Avignon for a few more years.

Section 4

Verbal Reasoning

Time – 35 Minutes

25 Questions

<u>Directions – Questions 1-13</u>: For each blank select one entry from the corresponding column of choices. Fill all blanks in the way that best completes the text.

---

1. They chalked their meeting up to _____; it was the kind of lucky thing that could never have happened by design.

a. preparation
b. serendipity
c. extravagance
d. peculiarity
e. concatenation

2. He was modest in his (i) _____ and did not (ii) _____ a promotion to higher levels of responsibility at work.

Blank (i)
a. dreams
b. habits
c. ambition

Blank (ii)
d. necessitate
e. pursue
f. refuse

3. History did not feel (i) _____ to her. Seeking a more (ii) _____ major she decided to study economics.

Blank (i)
a. esoteric
b. relevant
c. important

Blank (ii)
d. topical
e. sycophantic
f. trivial

4. She considered herself to be _____ and liked to predict events before they occurred.

a. precocious
b. prescient
c. predated
d. prefatory
e. preferential

5. "If the yeti is (i) _____", he asked, "then who made these (ii) _____ footprints?"

Blank (i)
a. imaginary
b. welcoming
c. mysterious

Blank (ii)
d. cavernous
e. unfathomable
f. colossal

6. Elijah noticed that the crowd had (i) _____ and it was possible once again to walk around the museum (ii) _____.

Blank (i)
a. startled
b. dispersed
c. intensified

Blank (ii)
d. with ease
e. convincingly
f. on foot

7. The trip was very (i) _____ and they vowed to each other that they would not take another for the (ii) _____ future.

Blank (i)
a. taxing
b. unpleasant
c. dignified

Blank (ii)
d. foreseeable
e. distant
f. so-called

8. In the same novel, Josephine Tey suggested that the truth about events in history becomes (i) _____ by perception and the passing of time when she indicated that incidences such as the Boston Massacre and the Tonypandy Riots in Wales did not occur as (ii) _____.

Blank (i)
a. amalgamated
b. obscured
c. featured

Blank (ii)
d. widely inspected
e. generally accepted
f. fully appreciated

9. The metaphysical poet John Donne lived a(n) _____ and colorful life: he wrote a range of earthy and seductive poems in his youth before becoming an Anglican priest and committing himself to composing the rich and exquisitely crafted Holy Sonnets.

a. indiscriminate
b. perplexing
c. discrete
d. diverse
e. resourceful

10. Although the history of the Knights Templar is filled with (i) _____ and intrigue, the founding of the order is far from mysterious or even dubious. In the year 1119, French Crusader Hugues de Payens created an order, to be known as the Knights Templar, to protect pilgrims to the Holy Land. Over the years the Knights Templar grew in wealth and (ii) _____ powerful connections with both church and state. Eventually, the Templars faced persecution for their acquired privilege, and in the 14th century the order was largely disbanded and lost power. Many since then have claimed a relationship between the modern-day Masons and the Templars of old, due to the Mason habit of (iii) _____ Templar imagery, but the idea is heavily rejected among authorities of both groups.

Blank (i)
a. deceit
b. symbolism
c. enigma

Blank (ii)
d. forged
e. manipulated
f. severed

Blank (iii)
g. adopting
h. alienating
i. approving

11. In Scotland, Rosslyn Chapel remains a (i) _____ for those who study both Masonic and Templar history. Construction of the chapel began in the 15th century and included many unusual symbolic elements whose meaning remains (ii) _____. Among these are engraved pillars, patterned carvings in the shape of 213 separate cubes, figures of what is believed to be corn, and gargoyle-like faces known as "green men."

Blank (i)
a. location of interest
b. place of worship
c. point of departure

Blank (ii)
d. unexceptional
e. unfamiliar
f. undetermined

12. The movie critic _____ the big-budget action film as overrated, badly performed, and lacking any substantial storyline.

a. detested
b. presented
c. lambasted
d. applauded
e. cautioned

13. Conscious that _____ often are lost in silent reading, the English teacher insisted on reading all poetry aloud to her class.

a. rhyme and style
b. genre and symbolism
c. nuance and metaphor
d. overall impact
e. rhythm and tone

Directions – Questions 14-21: Each passage in this group is followed by questions based on its content. After reading a passage, choose the best answer to each question. Answer all the questions following a passage on the basis of what is stated or implied in that passage.

Questions 14 through 18 are based on this passage.

The divide between the Christian churches of the East and those of the West went beyond a mere theological break and had broad social, political, and cultural effects. The event known as the Great Schism occurred in 1054, although some historians argue that it had been building for many years before this date and the final straw proved to be the addition of two words–*et filioque*–to the Nicene Creed. The expression was added to the Creed in the Western churches, and under the authority of the pope, but it was widely rebuked by the Eastern churches as lacking theological foundation. Additionally, the Roman Catholic Church in the West demanded that the Eastern Orthodox Church acknowledge the superior authority of Rome and the pope's infallibility. The Eastern leaders refused, and the schism was in effect.

It might seem that theological disputes have their place only in the church, but it is essential to consider the wide influence of the Christian church in medieval Europe. The church was the center of life and governed most aspects of it. Kings and emperors turned to the church for guidance. They ruled with the support of the church, and the church had only to remove that support to create a foundational weakness in the ruler's power. In the West, the pope was recognized as the infallible head of the church. The pope operated essentially as the mouthpiece of God for those under the authority of the Roman Catholic Church. The Eastern Orthodox Church, which operated under a recognizably fallible patriarch and a more regional system of bishops, rejected this outright. In breaking communion with the West, the East also broke the sense of accountability that each church had traditionally held toward the other. Broken communion also meant less cultural influence upon one another. Thus, the East and the West developed largely in isolation, and the divide between them spanned far more than geography and continues even to the modern day.

14. Based on the information in the passage, why did the church in the East object to the inclusion of the expression *et filioque*?

a. The expression, which is in Latin, did not reflect the liturgical language of the Eastern Orthodox Church.

b. The request from the pope for the title of supreme head of the church offended the Eastern Church and led them to reject the expression within the creed.

c. The church in the East was concerned that the church in the West was updating an ancient creed with the theological understanding of the day.

d. The church in the East believed that the expression altered the acknowledged understanding of scripture and thus was not acceptable.

e. The addition of *et filioque* to the Nicene Creed was simply the last in a long line of differences between the Eastern and Western churches and represented the final break.

Consider each of the three choices separately, and select all that apply.

15. Taking the information from the passage into account, why did the church in the East object to the pope in Rome being named supreme head of the Christian church?

a. The patriarch of the church in the East believed that he should hold the title of supreme head of the church.

b. Naming the pope as supreme head of the church would consolidate the Eastern churches under Western authority and undermine their own traditions.

c. The church in the East could not agree to acknowledge the pope as infallible.

16. Which of the following statements best describes the role of the Christian church in medieval Europe?

a. The Christian church offered citizens moral guidance for everyday life.

b. The Christian church provided moral direction to leaders and influenced their decision.

c. The Christian church was responsible for governing the people through its leaders.

For each of the following questions, select only one answer choice.

17. Based on the information in the passage, why might the church in the East object to acknowledging the infallibility of the pope in Rome?

a. The theological teachings of the church in the East claimed that no man could be infallible, thus nullifying the pope's own claim to infallibility.

b. As supreme head of the church, the pope would have the right to name and appoint all bishops to the churches in the East.

c. The relationship between the two churches provided accountability, but the pope's claim of infallibility would remove any need for accountability between East and West.

d. Based on the pope's claim of infallibility, the patriarch in the East felt obligated to excommunicate the pope in Rome and thus break off all communion between the churches.

e. The widening theological divide between the two churches meant that the East defined infallibility differently than the West, and the two could not agree on the correct definition.

18. Which of the following best summarizes the main point of the passage?

a. The Great Schism that occurred in 1054 had wide-ranging effects that were not limited to theological differences between East and West.

b. The Great Schism resulted after decades of conflict between the Eastern and Western churches and can still be felt today in theological differences between the churches.

c. The Great Schism isolated the East from the West and led to vast cultural differences between the two parts of Europe.

d. The Great Schism resulted in significant differences between the churches of the East and West but was probably inevitable given the distinctions already in place at the time.

e. The Great Schism had such an impact on the differences between the churches of the East and the West that leaders of each church have continued to excommunicate one another.

Questions 19 through 21 are based on this passage.

The question of global warming is one that cannot be answered easily, even by the scientists who devote their careers to studying global climate change. On one hand, these scientists have little doubt that the earth has experienced a warming trend over the last few decades. On the other hand, scientists do not agree entirely about whether or not this warming trend resulted from human activity, or particularly from greenhouse gas emissions. Some scientists have suggested that the increased warming is due to a natural cycle of climate change that will eventually end and reverse to a cooling phase. (In fact, these "mini ice ages" are not unknown in history; Europe recorded unusually low temperatures between the 13th century and the 16th century, thus explaining why so many paintings of monarchs such as Elizabeth I present her heavily clothed and even gloved.) Other scientists have raised questions about whether or not human greenhouse gas emissions could be enough to raise the entire temperature of the earth. These doubts aside, the consensus among scientific journals supports the theory of global warming from greenhouse gas emissions.

Consider each of the three choices separately, and select all that apply.

19. Based on the information in the passage, why do some scientists question the accuracy of human greenhouse gas emissions as the cause of global warming?

a. Scientists are unsure if humans can create enough greenhouse gas emissions to have an effect on worldwide climate.

b. Scientists believe that it is more likely the earth is experiencing a normal period of warming to be followed by a period of cooling.

c. Scientists believe that the causes of climate change are too complex to be limited to human activity.

20. Which of the following best describes the purpose of the parenthetical comment about the "mini ice age"?

a. The "mini ice age" explains why painted subjects in Elizabethan England were so often portrayed in heavy clothing and gloves.

b. The "mini ice age" conflicts with the evidence in scientific journals that widely supports the theory of greenhouse gas emissions.

c. The "mini ice age" represents a time when the earth experienced a normal climate cycle that altered global temperatures.

Select only one answer choice.

21. Which of the following best summarizes the meaning in the final sentence of the passage in the context of the entire passage?

a. Although scientific journals strongly support the theory of greenhouse gas emissions, an increasing number of scientists are beginning to doubt this idea.

b. Scientific journals refuse to acknowledge the questions that many scientists have about the cause of global warming.

c. Regardless of the questions that scientists have about the cause of global warming, the official line with scientific authorities supports the theory of greenhouse gas emissions.

d. The authors of scientific journals believe that there is enough evidence to support the theory of greenhouse gas emissions and a lack of evidence to support alternative theories.

e. The theory of greenhouse gas emissions has significant implications for political policy, so scientific journals feel obligated to acknowledge the theory as the official position.

Directions – Questions 22-25: Select the *two* answer choices that, when used to complete the sentence, fit the meaning of the sentence as a whole *and* produce completed sentences that are alike in meaning.

22. When the victim did not prove as _____ as expected, the blackmailer decided to resort to a more intense method of motivation.

a. sycophantic
b. patronizing
c. indolent
d. tractable
e. sardonic
f. amenable

23. The industrious third grade teacher was given a classroom full of _____ students, but by the end of the year they all received awards for good behavior.

    a. flagrant
    b. obstreperous
    c. boorish
    d. officious
    e. unruly
    f. sagacious

24. Sugar tends to weaken the immune system and will only _____ a problem, so patients recovering from illness are advised to stay away from sweets until fully recovered.

    a. belie
    b. ratify
    c. compound
    d. substantiate
    e. exacerbate
    f. opine

25. While the clergyman was extremely popular in the parish, the allegations of inappropriate behavior forced the leadership to _____ him of his position and send him to a purely administrative job.

    a. deliberate
    b. divest
    c. demolish
    d. decimate
    e. disconnect
    f. dispossess

Section 5

Quantitative Reasoning

Time – 40 minutes

SECTION 1: QUANTITATIVE COMPARISON

Directions: Compare Quantity A and Quantity B, using additional information centered above the two quantities if such information is given, and select one of the following four answer choices:

a. Quantity A is greater
b. Quantity B is greater
c. The two quantities are equal
d. The relationship cannot be determined from the information given

A symbol that appears more than once in a question has the same meaning throughout the question.

$$10^x = 10\ 000\ 000\ 000$$

	Quantity A	Quantity B	
1.	x	12	a. b. c. d.

Line A is represented by the following equation:
$$10y + 20x = 50$$

	Quantity A	Quantity B	
2.	The *y*-intercept of Line A	The slope of line A	a. b. c. d.

Figure **is not** drawn to scale

	Quantity A	Quantity B	
3.	$\frac{y}{x}$	3	a. b. c. d.

The following table displays the income Jane's business earned and the percentage of that income she paid in taxes for the first half of the year.

Month	Income earned ($)	Percentage paid in taxes (%)
January	10,000	10
February	50,000	30
March	20,000	20
April	10,000	10
May	30,000	20
June	90,000	40

	Quantity A	Quantity B	
4.	The average of the income tax Jane paid	22% of Jane's average income	a. b. c. d.

SECTION 2: MULTIPLE-CHOICE – SELECT ONLY ONE ANSWER CHOICE

5. If q is the smallest composite number greater than 2 and p is the smallest prime number less than 10, what is $\frac{p}{q}$?

    a. 0.5
    b. 1
    c. 2
    d. 4

Question 6 pertains to the following:

$$\frac{1}{25^n} > 1$$

6. For which value of n is the above statement true?

    a. $n = 1$
    b. $n = \sqrt{2}$
    c. $n = \frac{1}{2}$
    d. $n = -\frac{1}{2}$

Questions 7 – 9 pertain to the following diagram:

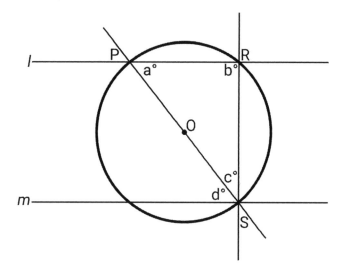

Figure **NOT** drawn to scale

Lines *l* and *m* are parallel. O is the center of the circle. The measure of angle d is 45°. The length of line RS is $\frac{\sqrt{2}}{2}$. Line RS forms a right angle with line *m*.

7. What is the measure of angle a?

    a. 30°
    b. 45°
    c. 60°
    d. 90°

8. What is the length of line PR?

    a. $\frac{\sqrt{2}}{2}$
    b. $\sqrt{2}$
    c. $2\sqrt{2}$
    d. 1

9. What is the diameter of circle O?

    a. 1
    b. $1\sqrt{2}$
    c. $2\sqrt{2}$
    d. $\frac{\sqrt{2}}{2}$

SECTION 3: MULTIPLE-CHOICE – SELECT ONE OR MORE ANSWER CHOICES

Directions: If the question specifies how many answer choices to select, select exactly that number of choices. If the question does not specify how many answer choices to select, select all that apply.

- The correct answer may be just one of the choices or may be as many as all of the choices
- No credit is given unless you select all of the correct choices and no others

10. Which two lines are parallel?

a. $y - 4x - 3 = 0$
b. $y - 2x - 3 = 0$
c. $4y - 12x - 16 = 0$
d. $3y - 9x + 18 = 0$

Question 11 pertains to the following equation:

$$\sqrt{x^2 + y^2} = 5$$

$$x^2 - y^2 = -7$$

11. If x and y satisfy the above system of equations, then which of the following are possible values for $x^3 + y^3$?

a. 21
b. 25
c. 37
d. 91

12. A square has vertices at the following four points: (0,0), (P,0), (0,P), and (P,P). Which of the following answers necessarily represent the perimeter of the square?

a. P^2
b. $P + P + P + P$
c. $(P)(P)$
d. $4P$

Questions 13 – 15 pertain to the following diagram:

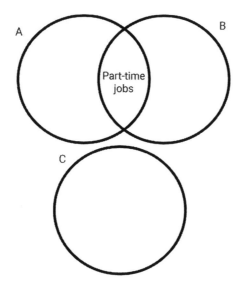

Figure **NOT** drawn to scale

Circle A represents students who major in liberal arts at a certain university. Circle B represents students who major in the life sciences at that university, and circle C represents engineering majors at the same university.

13. What does A∪B represent?

a. Only the subset of liberal arts and life science double-majors
b. All liberal arts and life science students
c. Only liberal arts students
d. Only life science students

14. What does A ∩ B represent?

a. The subset of liberal arts and life science double-majors
b. All liberal arts and life science students
c. Only liberal arts students
d. Only life science students

15. Why is circle C a disjoint set? Select all correct answers.

a. No engineering students are also liberal arts majors
b. No engineering students are also life science majors
c. No engineering students have part-time jobs
d. A small subset of engineering students double majored in liberal arts or life sciences

SECTION 4: NUMERIC ENTRY

Questions 16 – 20 pertain to the following:

Enter your answer as an integer or a decimal, rounded as instructed

John and Jane bought a house for $300,000. They put 20% down and took on a 30 year mortgage for the balance. The following graph represents the amount they paid towards the principle, interest, and taxes throughout the life of the loan. Use this information to answer questions 16 – 20.

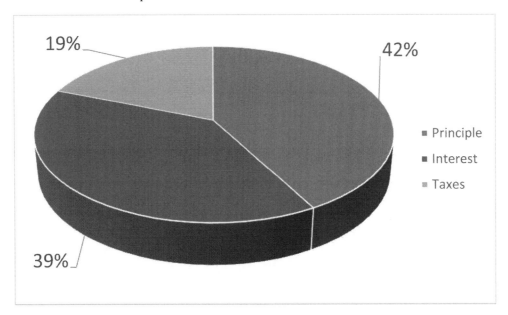

Figure: Breakdown of mortgage payments

16. What was the original amount of the loan?

$	0	0	0	0	0	0
	1	1	1	1	1	1
	2	2	2	2	2	2
	3	3	3	3	3	3
	4	4	4	4	4	4
	5	5	5	5	5	5
	6	6	6	6	6	6
	7	7	7	7	7	7
	8	8	8	8	8	8
	9	9	9	9	9	9

17. What is the total amount John and Jane will pay the bank at the end of their 30-year mortgage? Round your answer to the nearest dollar.

$	0	0	0	0	0	0
	1	1	1	1	1	1
	2	2	2	2	2	2
	3	3	3	3	3	3
	4	4	4	4	4	4
	5	5	5	5	5	5
	6	6	6	6	6	6
	7	7	7	7	7	7
	8	8	8	8	8	8
	9	9	9	9	9	9

18. By the end of their 30-year mortgage, what percentage of the original loan amount did they pay in interest? Round your answer to the nearest tenth of a percent.

.	.	.	.	.	.
0	0	0	0	0	0
1	1	1	1	1	1
2	2	2	2	2	2
3	3	3	3	3	3
4	4	4	4	4	4
5	5	5	5	5	5
6	6	6	6	6	6
7	7	7	7	7	7
8	8	8	8	8	8
9	9	9	9	9	9

19. What was their average annual interest rate? Round your answer to the nearest tenth of a percent.

.	.	.	.	.	.
0	0	0	0	0	0
1	1	1	1	1	1
2	2	2	2	2	2
3	3	3	3	3	3
4	4	4	4	4	4
5	5	5	5	5	5
6	6	6	6	6	6
7	7	7	7	7	7
8	8	8	8	8	8
9	9	9	9	9	9

20. How much did they pay in taxes by the end of the 30-year mortgage? Round your answer to the nearest dollar.

$	0	0	0	0	0	0
	1	1	1	1	1	1
	2	2	2	2	2	2
	3	3	3	3	3	3
	4	4	4	4	4	4
	5	5	5	5	5	5
	6	6	6	6	6	6
	7	7	7	7	7	7
	8	8	8	8	8	8
	9	9	9	9	9	9

Section 6

Quantitative Reasoning

Time – 40 minutes

Section 1: Quantitative Comparison

Directions: Compare Quantity A and Quantity B, using additional information centered above the two quantities if such information is given, and select one of the following four answer choices:

a. Quantity A is greater
b. Quantity B is greater
c. The two quantities are equal
d. The relationship cannot be determined from the information given

A symbol that appears more than once in a question has the same meaning throughout the question.

$$A \Psi B = (AB)^2 + (A + B)^2$$

	Quantity A	Quantity B	
1.	$2\Psi5$	150	a. b. c. d.

The electrical engineering department at a certain graduate school in the United States (US) has a total of 36 students. The department has twice as many male students as female students and three times as many international students as students who are US citizens.

	Quantity A	Quantity B	
2.	The number of students who are US citizens	The number of female students	a. b. c. d.

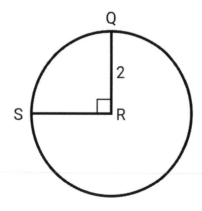

R is the center of the circle below:
Figure **NOT** drawn to scale

	Quantity A	Quantity B	
3.	Half the circumference of the circle	The area of triangle QRS	a. b. c. d.

The graph below shows the gross domestic product (GDP) in trillions of US dollars for four countries between 2000 and 2008.

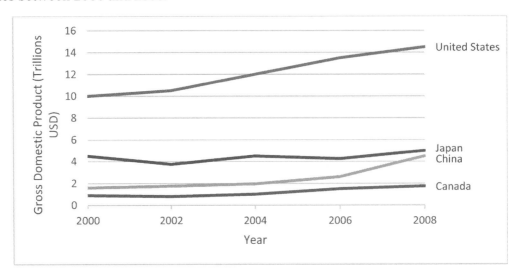

	Quantity A	Quantity B	
4.	The combined GDP of Japan, China, and Canada in 2008	The GDP of the US in 2008	a. b. c. d.

SECTION 2: MULTIPLE-CHOICE – SELECT ONLY ONE ANSWER CHOICE

5. The graduating class at a certain university has 100 students. Within that class, 60% of the students are male. 30% of the class will attend graduate school in computer science in the fall. Of the students who will attend graduate school in computer science, the ratio of males to females is 2:1. What percentage of the female students in the graduating class will attend graduate school in computer science?

    a. 10%
    b. 20%
    c. 25%
    d. 75%

Questions 6 pertains to the following equation:

$$\text{The equation for Line Q is } 5y - 100x - 75 = 0.$$

6. Which line below has a slope that is twice the slope of Line Q?

    a. Line A: $y - 20x - 15 = 0$
    b. Line B: $y - 40x - 15 = 0$
    c. Line C: $2y - 40x - 30 = 0$
    d. Line D: $2y - 20x - 15 = 0$

Questions 7 – 10 pertain to the following table:

Table: May 2010 occupational wage estimates for California

Occupational category	Median hourly wage (US dollars)	Mean hourly wage (US dollars)	Mean annual wage (US dollars)
Management	50.67	57.44	119,480
Legal	47.22	57.27	119,120
Computers and mathematics	40.66	42.30	87,980
Education, training, and library	25.18	27.89	58,010
Food preparation and related services	9.28	10.57	21,990

7. If there were only four managers in the state of California, which list below could represent their hourly wages?

    a. $50.67, $50.67, $50.67, $50.67
    b. $57.44, $57.44, $57.44, $57.44
    c. $48.25, $50.57, $50.77, $80.18
    d. $50.67, $50.67, $57.44, $57.44

8. Which of these is the smallest percentage that the mean wage would have to increase for those who work in computers and mathematics to earn more on average annually than those who work in management?

    a. 32%
    b. 33%
    c. 35%
    d. 36%

9. Assume a short order cook earns the mean hourly wage for his standard shift and when working overtime. How many hours of weekly overtime must he work to earn approximately the mean annual salary of a librarian. The standard work schedule is 40 hours per week, 52 weeks per year.

    a. 106
    b. 66
    c. 46
    d. 40

10. A junior associate lawyer at a top law firm currently earns the mean annual income for working 40 hours per week, 52 weeks per year. In addition to her annual salary, she also earns the mean hourly wage for each hour of the ten overtime hours she averages weekly. She was recently offered a promotion to senior associate, a position that comes with a 25% increase in annual salary but which offers no overtime compensation. Considering that senior associates typically work 55 hours per week, would the promotion be to the lawyer's financial advantage?

    a. Yes
    b. No
    c. Not enough information

SECTION 3: MULTIPLE-CHOICE – SELECT ONE OR MORE ANSWER CHOICES

If the question specifies how many answer choices to select, select exactly that number of choices.

If the question does not specify how many answer choices to select, select all that apply.

- The correct answer may be just one of the choices or may be as many as all of the choices.
- No credit is given unless you select all of the correct choices and no others.

11. **Which two numbers have a product of A^{11} and a possible quotient of A^7?**

    a. A^2
    b. A^3
    c. A^6
    d. A^9

Questions 12 – 13 pertain to the following figure:

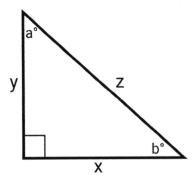

Figure **NOT** drawn to scale

12. **If z = 3, indicate all answers that could be the length of x.**

    a. 1
    b. 2
    c. 3
    d. 4

13. **If $\frac{b}{a} = 2$ and x = 1, then what are possible values for z?**

    a. 1
    b. 2
    c. 3
    d. 4

14. **Jack, Jill, and John are siblings. Jack is twice as old as Jill and half as old as John. If the ages of all three siblings are contained within the answer choices, how old could Jill be?**

    a. 2
    b. 4
    c. 8
    d. 16

15. A triangle has vertices at points (0,0), (0,3), and (4,0). Which of the following are lengths of the triangle's sides?

    a. 2
    b. 3
    c. 5
    d. 7

SECTION 4: NUMERIC ENTRY

Directions: Enter your answer as an integer or a decimal, rounded as instructed.

Questions 16 – 20 pertain to the following figure:

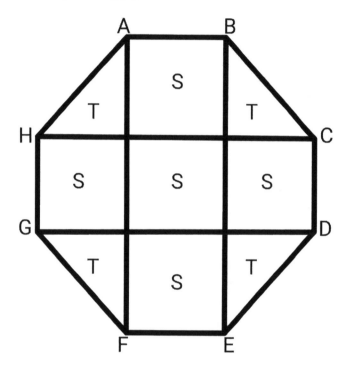

Figure **NOT** drawn to scale

Octagon ABCDEFGH contains five squares (S) and four triangles (T). The length of side AB is 6.

16. What is the sum of the areas the five squares S?

.	.	.	.	.	.
0	0	0	0	0	0
1	1	1	1	1	1
2	2	2	2	2	2
3	3	3	3	3	3
4	4	4	4	4	4
5	5	5	5	5	5
6	6	6	6	6	6
7	7	7	7	7	7
8	8	8	8	8	8
9	9	9	9	9	9

17. What is the length of side BC? Round your answer to nearest tenth.

.	.	.	.	.	.
0	0	0	0	0	0
1	1	1	1	1	1
2	2	2	2	2	2
3	3	3	3	3	3
4	4	4	4	4	4
5	5	5	5	5	5
6	6	6	6	6	6
7	7	7	7	7	7
8	8	8	8	8	8
9	9	9	9	9	9

18. What is the area of a single triangle T?

.	.	.	.	.	.
0	0	0	0	0	0
1	1	1	1	1	1
2	2	2	2	2	2
3	3	3	3	3	3
4	4	4	4	4	4
5	5	5	5	5	5
6	6	6	6	6	6
7	7	7	7	7	7
8	8	8	8	8	8
9	9	9	9	9	9

19. What is the perimeter of octagon ABCDEFGH? Round your answer to nearest tenth.

.	.	.	.	.	.
0	0	0	0	0	0
1	1	1	1	1	1
2	2	2	2	2	2
3	3	3	3	3	3
4	4	4	4	4	4
5	5	5	5	5	5
6	6	6	6	6	6
7	7	7	7	7	7
8	8	8	8	8	8
9	9	9	9	9	9

20. What is the area of octagon ABCDEFGH?

.	.	.	.	.	.
0	0	0	0	0	0
1	1	1	1	1	1
2	2	2	2	2	2
3	3	3	3	3	3
4	4	4	4	4	4
5	5	5	5	5	5
6	6	6	6	6	6
7	7	7	7	7	7
8	8	8	8	8	8
9	9	9	9	9	9

Answer Key

Verbal Reasoning				Quantitative Reasoning			
Section 3		Section 4		Section 5		Section 6	
Number	Answer	Number	Answer	Number	Answer	Number	Answer
1	B, F	1	B	1	B	1	B
2	A, E	2	C, E	2	A	2	B
3	A, D	3	B, D	3	C	3	A
4	B, D	4	B	4	A	4	B
5	C, D	5	A, F	5	A	5	C
6	B, F	6	B, D	6	D	6	B
7	E	7	A, D	7	B	7	C
8	B, D, H	8	B, E	8	A	8	D
9	A, E, I	9	D	9	A	9	B
10	C	10	C, D, G	10	C, D	10	B
11	C	11	A, F	11	C, D	11	A, D
12	B	12	C	12	B, D	12	A, B
13	D	13	E	13	B	13	B
14	A	14	D	14	A	14	A, B
15	E	15	B, C	15	A, B, C	15	B, C
16	A, C	16	A, B	16	240,000	16	180
17	B	17	C	17	571,429	17	8.5
18	B	18	A	18	92.90%	18	18
19	D	19	A	19	3.10%	19	58
20	B, E	20	C	20	108,572	20	252
21	A, F	21	D				
22	C, D	22	D, F				
23	B, D	23	B, E				
24	B	24	C, E				
25	E	25	B, F				

Answer Explanations

Section 3

Verbal Reasoning

1. B, F: The correct answer is choice B (address) and choice F (intricacies).

2. A, E: The correct answer is choice A (brief) and choice E (characters).

3. A, D: The correct answer is choice A (fabricated) and choice D (refute).

4. B, D: The correct answer is choice B (condition) and choice D (despondent).

5. C: Answers (A) and (E) are incorrect because they suggest the disarray was minor; the opposite of the meaning suggested by the rest of the sentence. Answers (B) and (D) are incorrect because they offer information about the disarray that is not relevant to the rest of the sentence.

6. B, F: The correct answer is choice B (boisterous) and choice F (overwhelm).

7. E: All the adjectives describing the house and the things in the house suggest a showy and grandiose home; ostentatious is the only answer choice that fits this meaning.

8. B, D, H: The tone of the passage is one of contrast, primarily the contrast in the friendship between the young Prince Hal and the man who becomes King Henry V. The first part of the sentence should indicate the strength of the friendship, while the second part should indicate both Falstaff's failure to grow up as Hal does and the subsequent results of Falstaff's failure. Answer choice A (preferred) indicates an option for the first blank, but it does not provide the sense of importance about the relationship. Falstaff's friendship was not just preferred; rather, it was cherished. The second blank has to indicate the disparity between Falstaff and Hal as the latter grows into King Henry, and the best contrast to the phrase "youthful antics" is to describe the new king as "maturing." Finally, the last blank has to suggest that the differences between them have led to a breach in friendship. Nothing in the passage suggests that Hal/Henry tries to reform his friend, and as a result the passage seems to imply that the former friendship cannot be restored.

Thus, the correct answers are choice B (cherished), choice D (maturing), and choice H (renounce).

9. A, E, I: Determining the correct answers to question 2 requires reading the entire passage and appreciating all of its suggestions before attempting to fill in any of the blanks. For the first blank, two answer choices can be eliminated immediately. Answer choice B (utterly detestable) is largely an opinion statement with no support within the passage, while answer choice C faces contrast from the later portions of the passage. (If King Richard III is not actually guilty of the crime, then he can hardly be described as "consistently suspicious.") He can, however, be described as "popularly malevolent," if his guilt has always been presumed among the general population. For the second blank, the best option will indicate that a theory has been proposed, and the closest word to this is "propounded." What is more, neither of the other answer choices makes any sense. Finally, the third blank should indicate correctly that King Richard III's successor King Henry VII went back in time, so to speak, to give the impression that his predecessor committed the crime. The best answer choice for this blank is "retrospectively." No doubt Henry also did these things eagerly and

103

intentionally, but the former word is impossible to determine within the context of the sentence, and the second word feels redundant without adding anything to the sentence.

Thus, the correct answers are choice A (popularly malevolent), choice E (propounded), and choice I (retrospectively).

10. C: In the first sentence, the author notes the following: "It might be surprising to discover that Europe's first republic pre-dated the turn of the 11th century, long before Europe would see the rise of another such system." This statement clearly indicates that Iceland's republic came well before another in Europe, so indeed it was "many years" before another republic emerged in Europe. The author of the passage mentions a monarchy in Norway and Denmark, but this mention alone is not enough to assume that monarchy was the more common system–based only on the information in the passage. The information in answer choices B and D focuses solely on the republic in Iceland, and this counters the question with its focus on the development of republics in Europe. Additionally, the author mentions that Iceland is currently a republic, but this mention alone is not enough to comment on modern republics in Europe or on the level of "sophistication" that defines them.

11. C: The last two statements in the passage state the following: "This system, and Iceland's identity as a republic, remained in place until 1262, when the decision of the Althing agreed to the Old Covenant and placed Iceland under the authority of the king of Norway. Iceland would not become a self-governing republic again until 1944, when the people of Iceland voted to end their political relationship with the kingdom of Denmark." As Norway and Denmark are definitely different nations, the author fails to explain how (and when) Iceland came to be part of Denmark; the lack of information creates confusion for the reader. Answers choice A and B contain information that, while potentially interesting, offer nothing of substantial value to the topic of the passage. It is not necessary to know when Iceland converted to Christianity, and there is little use in digging deeper to find out why settlers left Norway and went to Iceland in the first place.

12. B: It stands to reason that if the 13th century agreement became known as the Old Covenant, there must have been a later covenant to follow. However, the question specifically asks for implication of mentioning the Althing in relation to the Old Covenant, so the information about a later covenant ultimately is irrelevant to the question. At the same time, the mention of the Althing indicates that the freemen of Iceland, who did have a voice in their government, were involved in the decision in some fashion. Answer choice C creates the potential for a correct option, but it contains information that cannot be inferred clearly from the passage: the free men of Iceland might have had some say in the decision of the Old Covenant, but it is impossible to determine from the passage if they ultimately resisted the union.

13. D: The Althing was largely a legislative body with a degree of judicial authority. The role of the Lawspeaker was to oversee the Althing, read the laws, moderate disputes, and oversee the assembly. This role is ultimately similar to the role of the Speaker of the House within the U.S. House of Representatives, who oversees the activities of the House and moderates when necessary. The Lawspeaker had a much lesser role than that of the President or of a Lieutenant Governor (who acts in a role similar to the Vice President, but within a state instead of at the federal level). The President of the Senate oversees the Senate and casts the occasional tie-breaking vote but has nowhere near the same presence or the role as the Speaker of the House. The Secretary of State is largely a bureaucratic position with political responsibilities, but it does not offer a comparative position to the Lawspeaker.

14. A: The author notes that the purpose of the Althing was "to discuss and determine legal issues." In addition, the first sentence points out that the Althing "represented an important development in making the people of a nation an active part of the system that governed them." This statement clearly matches the information in answer choice A, that the Althing's purpose was to "determine the laws of Iceland and to provide the free men with a role in their government." While the Althing might have contributed to creating a stable government in Iceland, that is not its purpose as noted in the passage. The author points out that the Althing called together the leaders from each community, but nothing in the passage suggests that the Althing developed leaders or attempted to make the communities self-governing. Additionally, the author of the passage says nothing about uniting the citizenry against foreign powers. And while it might be inferred that the Althing contributed to developing consistent application of the laws, this answer choice does not offer as good a summary as the information in answer choice A.

15. E: Early in the passage, the author says, "Most grains contain phytic acid, which can prevent proper mineral absorption. For instance, phytic acid can block the body's ability to absorb iron from foods and thus raise the potential over time for anemia." This statement matches the information in answer choice E. The author says nothing about phytic acid binding with the minerals; instead, the author explains that phytic acid blocks mineral absorption. The author does not discuss the amount of phytic acid within other foods; as the passage only discusses phytic acid within grains, there is no way to determine if the amount in grains is higher than in other foods (or if phytic acid is found in other foods at all). The passage mentions both phytic acid and gluten, and the author points out that reducing the phytic acid can make glutinous grains easier to digest for those persons with gluten-intolerance; but this assertion is not enough to make the leap that phytic acid attaches itself to gluten. Finally, the passage makes no claim about phytic acid attacking the body's digestive system; rather, it seems that the harm is more passive.

16. A, C: The author provides a two-part reason for soaking grains: soaking the grains reduces the amount of phytic acid within them and thus makes them easier for the body to digest. The author makes no mention about whether or not soaking grains removes the gluten, so answer choice B cannot be a correct option.

17. B: Food science is mentioned without definition within the passage, but the information provided about phytic acid and the comments from food scientists regarding the soaking of grains provide enough detail for inference. Based on the information in the passage, it can safely be said that a food scientist considers the chemicals in food and analyzes the properties of those chemicals. The passage does not offer enough information to indicate that food science is related solely to food preparation, particularly since phytic acid is an ingredient in grains prior to their preparation. The passage is based primarily on a chemical within grains, but the claim that food science is limited entirely to grains is too narrow. If this were the case, the field would likely be called grain science, instead of food science. The passage mentions people preparing their grains at home, but it mentions nothing about the commercial preparation of food, so it cannot be said that food science is limited to domestic food preparation. The author makes no mention of the use of modern technology, so answer choice D cannot be inferred from the passage.

18. B: The Spanish cannot attack a colony if they are unaware of its location. Historical documents indicating that the Spanish government had not yet discovered the location of Roanoke would certainly lend credence to the claims of historians "who argue conflicting evidence" regarding the theory of Spanish attack. Colonies can be attacked by more ways than just gunfire, so the idea that archeologists cannot find ammunition represents weak evidence against a Spanish attack. Answer choice C offers an option that does more to support the idea of Spanish attack rather than offering evidence to conflict with it. Answer choice D combines ideas in the paragraph but also confuses them; the author notes that Chief Powhatan "claimed responsibility for their deaths, because the colonists allied themselves with a tribe that did not support him." It makes little sense then for him to claim to have killed the Roanoke colonists if he was working to forge a treaty that would protect them. The author of the passage clearly negates the theory about a cannibal attack, so answer choice E cannot be correct.

19. D: The first sentence of the passage provides a strong clue about the substance of the passage: "The mystery of Roanoke Colony has never been solved to any satisfaction, although a number of theories have arisen over the years." In other words, there are many theories about what happened at Roanoke Colony, but not enough evidence exists to prove the validity of any of them. The author mentions the information in answer choice A as one of the theories but does not claim it as the best or most likely. The information in the passage would suggest a measure of disagreement among historians, but "complete disagreement" cannot be inferred; furthermore, this hardly can be described as the main point of the passage. Answer choice C offers an alternative not provided, or implied, within the passage and as a result cannot represent a summary of the main point. Answer choice E takes details from the passage and remixes them to some extent, but this information cannot be inferred and clearly is not the main point of the passage.

20. B, E: The sentence implies that the student is unprepared for the information in the course; a prerequisite is a course required or encouraged before another course is taken. A prerequisite tends to offer the information a student needs to be prepared for increasingly complex information in the course that follows. This would suggest that, without the information, the student does not know how to appreciate the shades of meaning within the poetry.

Thus, the correct answer choices are choice B (nuance) and choice E (subtlety). The words *counterfeit, presumption,* and *pariah* make little sense within the context of the sentence. The word *resonance* can be applied to poetry, but it does not fit the suggestion that the student lacks the necessary background to understand the complexity of the information being presented.

21. A, F: If the couple plans to live within a budget, then likely the couple plans to reduce any unnecessary spending and focus only on their basic needs. The implication is that extra spending–spending that is excessive or not essential to their absolute requirements–will end. This indicates that they are eliminating superfluous or irrelevant expenditures.

Thus, the correct answer choices are choice A (superfluous) and choice F (irrelevant). Something that is indispensable is necessary, so answer choice B expresses the very opposite of the implied meaning. The word *unequivocal* means definite, so this word does not fit the meaning of the sentence. Additionally, the words *indifferent* and *paramount* offer little to the meaning of the sentence.

22. C, D: The sentence seems to suggest that the vehicle manufacturer had advertised a very large trunk, but the reality proved to be the opposite of this claim. Additionally, the opening word *although* provides a sense of contrast between the small trunk space and the expectation of something larger. The correct answer choice options will indicate great size or a large amount of space. As a result, the only possible correct answers are *capacious* and *commodious.*

Thus the correct answers are choice C (capacious) and choice D (commodious). Something ostentatious is flamboyant or showy, and while such words can describe some vehicles, these words hardly offer a solid contrast to the reality of the trunk size. The words *inadvertent, palatable,* and *analogous* make no sense in the context of the sentence or in contrast to the small size of the trunk.

23. B, D: The context of the sentence indicates that the woman represents the man's perfect image of beauty. There is a further indication of contrast between this image he has carried in his head and the reality of the changes in her over the years. As a result, the answers must present her as his highest ideal from years before. She is not merely a pretty girl he remembers; instead, she represents the highest standard of beauty upon which all others are judged.

Thus, the correct answers are choice B (exemplar) and choice D (archetype). The word *conjecture*, meaning guess, makes no sense in the context of the sentence. The word *precedent* suggests a previously established example. While she is the precedent for his standard, she is more of a paradigm than a mere precedent. The words *malefactor* and *dilettante* have no place in the sentence.

24. B: The second sentence of the passage notes the following: "Unlike the earlier schism, though, this Western Schism resulted from political disputes among the factions within the church." This statement clearly indicates that the primary difference was the result of internal conflict and political disagreements. The author mentions that the church moved from Rome to Avignon due to a "period of crisis." This is not part of the author's statement about the differences between the East-West split and the Western Schism, however. Additionally, the author mentions that the cardinals viewed their selection of Pope Urban VI as a bad idea, but this falls under the idea of internal conflict and even political disagreements. Furthermore, it is an incidental part of the larger problem(s) that arose. The question is looking for information about the larger problem(s)–as this is what distinguishes the two splits–so answer choice C is too narrow in focus.

25. E: The final sentence reads as follows: "Order returned with the election of Pope Martin V in 1417, although Avignon continued a feeble resistance until 1429." This statement indicates that the appointment of Pope Martin V was widely accepted in Europe and not disputed among the cardinals, but that Avignon resisted by retaining a different claimant until 1429. Answer choice A explains the first part of the sentence but fails to explain the second part about the "feeble resistance" in Avignon. Answer choice B attempts to reconcile what appears an inconsistency in the passage. But the information in the passage would indicate that historians correctly recognize that the Western Schism ended in 1417, even though Avignon continued to do its own thing for a few years. Apparently, the appointment of Pope Martin V was enough to provide an acceptable conclusion to the split for most parties involved. The author makes no attempt to explain *why* Pope Martin V was generally acceptable, and given that Avignon did continue to resist for a few more years it would stand to reason that he did not have connections here. Answer choice D reiterates information from the passage but fails entirely to answer the question.

Section 4

Verbal Reasoning

1. B: The word sought is one that describes something lucky that does not happen through design. Answer (B), serendipity, fits this meaning. Answer (A) is incorrect as it means the opposite of the word sought. Answers (C), (D) and (E) do not relate to the rest of the sentence.

2. C, E: The correct answer is choice C (ambition) and choice E (pursue).

3. B, D: The correct answer is choice B (relevant) and choice D (topical).

4. B: The correct answer is (B) prescient, which means able to anticipate the course of events. Choice (A) means early in development and is incorrect. Choice (C) means preceding in time and is incorrect. Choice (D) means related to a preface or located in front and is incorrect. Choice (E) means showing preference and is incorrect.

5. A, F: The correct answer is choice A (imaginary) and choice F (colossal).

6. B, D: The correct answer is choice B (dispersed) and choice D (with ease).

7. A, D: The correct answer is choice A (taxing) and choice D (foreseeable).

8. B, E: The first blank of this sentence should indicate the changes that can occur with the understanding of events in history. The author of the passage mentions the ideas of "perception" and "passage of time," both of which suggest that the truth can be difficult (or even impossible) to see clearly. The best option, then, is the word "obscured." It is worth mentioning that neither answer choice A nor answer choice C makes much sense in the context. For the second blank, the best answer choice will suggest the perception noted in the first part of the sentence, that is, the perception of the way that events occurred. This perception correctly could be described as "generally accepted." The phrase "fully appreciated" has potential, but it does not quite work with the statement about truth being obscured; something can hardly be appreciated in full if the information about it is not entirely correct. The phrase "widely inspected," on the other hand, offers nothing of value to the sentence and can be eliminated immediately.

Thus, the correct answers are choice B (obscured) and choice E (generally accepted).

9. D: The passage describes the life and poetry of John Donne, and particularly his divergent interests. The correct answer will thus express this divergence, and it must do so within the bounds of the information presented. Additionally, the word needs to work alongside the description "colorful." The only solid answer then is "diverse." Answer choice A (indiscriminate) represents a judgment statement not supported by the information in the sentence. Answer choice B (perplexing) indicates a potential impression on the part of the reader, but this word is not appropriate as an answer choice for the sentence. Answer choice C (discrete) suggests the detachment between the first part of Donne's life and the second, but it does not work well alongside the description "colorful," which indicates that Donne had varying interests that enriched his life, rather than that he made a sharp break between one stage of life and another. Finally, answer choice E (resourceful) has no immediate support within the sentence, so it should be eliminated as an option.

Thus, the correct answer is choice D (diverse).

10. C, D, G: Although the test-taker would be well advised to read the entire passage before attempting to fill in the blank, this question does not necessarily require such an action. The sentence can be completed blank by blank, without any of the meaning being lost. In the first blank, it is essential to sense the contrast between the first part of the sentence and the second. The word in the blank is set alongside the word "intrigue" and then contrasted with the words "mysterious or even dubious." Since the nature of intrigue tends to be questionable (and thus dubious), this would suggest that the first blank should encapsulate the idea of mystery. The best option then is "enigma." The word "deceit" functions as a synonym for "intrigue" and is thus redundant. The word "symbolism" offers nothing to the contrast. For the second blank, it is necessary to decide which verb makes the most sense in explaining the Templars and their connections. Based on the context, the Templars expanded in both wealth and connections, so the verb should be positive in this sense. The best choice, therefore, is "forged." There is not enough information in the passage to suggest–in this specific case–that the Templars "manipulated" connections (nor does this make a great deal of sense in the context), and the word "severed" suggests exactly the opposite of what is implied in the sentence. The final blank should offer some explanation for why a connection has been assumed between Masons and Templars. It makes no sense for Masons to "alienate" imagery, and there is not enough in the idea of "approving" it to justify this answer choice. The best option then is "adopting." The use of Templar imagery adopted into Masonic ritual would certainly lead some people to believe in a potential connection.

Thus, the correct answers are choice C (enigma), choice D (forged), and choice G (adopting).

11. A, F: The first blank in question 6 must identify the perception of Rosslyn Chapel among those persons interested in Masonic and Templar history. The place may be a chapel, but there is little information in the entire passage to suggest that historians go there as a "place of worship." Additionally, there is not enough information to indicate how it would be a "point of departure," so the best (and only) answer choice has to be "location of interest." What is more, the details in the rest of the passage explain why–that is, the unusual design elements. In the second blank, it is necessary to determine how these design elements are perceived. It makes no sense for their meaning to be "unexceptional," particularly given the description of them that follows. While they are certainly "unfamiliar" in some ways, it is more difficult to describe their actual meaning this way. The option "undetermined," offers a clear and effective word choice, so this word is the correct answer.

Thus, the correct answers are choice A (location of interest) and choice F (undetermined).

12. C: The appropriate word choice will indicate that the movie critic did not care for the film, since the summary of the review offers nothing in the way of a positive opinion. In addition, the correct answer choice also will encapsulate what would be a standard movie-reviewing idea. Clearly, the reviewer detested the film, but this is not enough. A reviewer offers more than just an opinion about whether or not he/she liked the film. The review itself is a description of the film's qualities and what influences these qualities. Answer choice A (detested) is only half of the reviewing equation, so it is not enough. Answer choice B (presented) could work, but it does not have the necessary negative connotation that the details of the review require. Answer choice C (lambasted) makes the most sense, as it indicates both the negative perception of the film and the active explanation about what is wrong with it. Answer choice D (applauded) conflicts with the description of the film and makes no sense. Answer choice E (cautioned) works only if the reviewer is cautioning filmgoers against the movie, but as this is not occurring it does not fit the context.

Thus, the correct answer is choice C (lambasted).

13. E: The correct answer choice in this question will indicate what is gained in poetic reading aloud versus a silent reading of poetry. Rhyme and style (answer choice A) are present in both cases, with a limited gain in understanding rhyme from reading aloud. Genre and symbolism (answer choice B) are also present, and the same can be said for nuance and metaphor (answer choice C). Overall impact (answer choice D) does not work, because the plural verb requires two options instead of one. Rhythm and tone (answer choice E), however, are heavily influenced by pronunciation, and some of this can be lost in a silent reading.

Thus, the correct answer is choice E (rhythm and tone).

14. D: In the first paragraph, the author notes that the expression *et filioque* "was widely rebuked by the Eastern churches as lacking theological foundation." This statement corresponds with the answer choice claiming that the Eastern Church believed that the expression altered the acknowledged understanding of scripture and was thus unacceptable to them. Answer choice A, claiming that the church in the East rejected the inclusion of a Latin phrase has no justification in the passage, because the author makes no comment about standard liturgical languages among the different churches. Answer choice B is irrelevant, because it discusses the request by the pope to be named supreme head of the Church, instead of the *et filioque* dispute. Answer choice C includes information that cannot be inferred from the passage; there is not enough detail in the passage to claim that the addition of *et filioque* reflected theological understanding of the day. Answer choice E simply summarizes the issue as explained in the first paragraph but does not effectively explain *why*.

15. B, C: In the second paragraph, the author notes the following: "The Eastern Orthodox Church, which operated under a recognizably fallible patriarch and a more regional system of bishops, rejected this outright." This statement suggests two things. First, the church in the East operated under its own (long-accepted) traditions, with the move by the pope thus placing the church in the East under the church in the West and undermining these traditions. Additionally, it implies that the church in the East, which believed its primary leader (the patriarch) to be fallible, would not be able to acknowledge infallibility in the pope. The author of the passage says nothing about a move by the patriarch to be named supreme head; furthermore, this actually takes away from the statement about the traditions in the East, so it cannot be correct.

16. A, B: The author makes the following statements in the second paragraph: "The church was the center of life and governed most aspects of it. Kings and emperors turned to the church for guidance. They ruled with the support of the church, and the church had only to remove that support to create a foundational weakness in the ruler's power." Of the answer choices, two can be derived from this statement. On the one hand, the church offered the people of medieval Europe guidance for everyday life. On the other hand, the church gave moral direction to leaders and influenced their decisions. The author does suggest that the church's influence could be extended to making or breaking kings, but there is not enough information in the passage to make the claim that the church governed *through* leaders. (In many cases, this statement was more or less true, but the passage does not go this far, so answer choice C cannot be correct.)

17. C: The author states, "The Eastern Orthodox Church, which operated under a recognizably fallible patriarch and a more regional system of bishops, rejected this outright. In breaking communion with the West, the East also broke the sense of accountability that each church had traditionally held toward the other." This statement suggests that the communion between the churches offered a degree of accountability, even though the pope was seen as infallible in the West. (The fact that he was not seen this way in the East would necessarily undermine the idea to some degree and maintain an ongoing sense of accountability between the churches.) When the pope asked that the East accept him as the infallible head of the church, the accountability that head developed over the centuries would more or less vanish, and the church in the East would find itself operating under the church in the West instead of working alongside it. Answer choice A might have truth in it, particularly since the author does note that the Eastern Church did not recognize infallibility in its patriarch, but this is not as strong an answer choice as choice C. It takes a more simplistic look at the issue but fails to acknowledge the broader implication of accepting infallibility in the pope. Similarly, answer choice B likely is true, but it fails to consider the larger issue of accountability that the author mentions clearly in the passage. The question that should follow answer choice B is *why* the East might object to this, and the correct answer choice will, not surprisingly, answer questions instead of raise them. Answer choice D offers details not contained within the passage, so it cannot be correct. (This is in fact true: the patriarch excommunicated the pope, and the pope returned the favor. But the author does not mention this, so the information is irrelevant as an answer choice.) Answer choice E also brings up information not within the passage; the author does not indicate in any place that the churches defined "fallible/infallible" a certain way, so this answer choice cannot be correct.

18. A: The first sentence of the first paragraph reads as follows: "The divide between the Christian churches of the East and those of the West went beyond a mere theological break and had broad social, political, and cultural effects." This statement summarizes the overall thrust of the passage, and answer choice A offers a clear restatement of this. Answer choice B summarizes the last sentence of the paragraph but fails to include the information about the broader effects of the Great Schism (with regards to social, political, and cultural effects). Answer choice C offers a more skeletal version of answer choice A, but it is not as strong an option and feels vague in focus. It also focuses only on the cultural differences and fails to take into account the social and political effects that the author mentions. Answer choice D infers information not necessarily stated in the passage; the author does not claim that the Great Schism was inevitable, so it is impossible to read this as a summary of the passage. Additionally, answer choice E mentions excommunication, which the author does not mention, so it too fails as a solid summary of the passage.

19. A: The author notes within the passage that scientists have questioned the theory of greenhouse gas emissions as contributing to global warming on two counts: (1) periods of warming might be part of natural temperature cycles on the earth, and (2) scientists cannot agree if humans can produce enough greenhouse gases to exert such a massive effect on global temperature. The first of these options is not among the answer choices; the second is, so that is the only correct answer choice. Answer choice B is connected to the idea of a period of global warming, but it infers too much with the claim that scientists believe this; in fact, the author only notes that scientists have pointed out the possibility. The author says nothing about scientists believing that the causes of global climate change are too complex for human involvement, so answer choice C cannot be correct.

20. C: Question 20 asks for the "purpose" of the parenthetical comment in the passage. Taken in context, there really is just one purpose: to explain that periods of widespread climate change do occur and have occurred in earth's history. The mention of heavy clothing and gloves in the Elizabethan period is more of a point of interest but in reality, has little to do with the main point of the passage; it certainly does not explain the purpose of the parenthetical comment within the passage. The author does not go so far as to say that the information about "mini ice ages" conflicts with the theory espoused by scientific journals. It might, but it also might be that the scientific journals have taken this into account. Without further information, answer choice B cannot describe the purpose of the parenthetical comment.

21. C: The final sentence of the passage states the following: "These doubts aside, the consensus among scientific journals supports the theory of global warming from greenhouse gas emissions." In other words, for now the official statement among scientific journals accepts the theory of global warming as a result of greenhouse gas emissions. Science is an evolving field, and scientists are always studying data and offering updates where appropriate. It is not surprising that some scientists have questions about this official theory, but it is also not surprising that scientific journals currently present the theory as official. Until solid evidence suggests otherwise, the official theory will hold. Answer choice A indicates part of the information in the passage, but it leans too far in inferring details from the author. The author suggests scientists continue to study this matter; the author says nothing about an increasing number doubting the official theory. The author says nowhere that scientific journals refuse to acknowledge the questions that scientists have, so answer choice B also infers too much. The final sentence indicates that scientific journals, for now, are confident about their claims. This might indicate that the authors of these journals believe in strong evidence to support the official theory and a lack of evidence to support alternative theories. The problem with this statement, however, is its inference based on the final sentence, rather than a summary of the final sentence. So, answer choice D is not a good option. Nowhere in the passage does the author mention political policy, least of all in the final sentence, so answer choice E cannot be correct.

22. D, F: The sentence suggests that the blackmailer had expected the victim to be easier to work with and more malleable to his plans. There is a hint of contrast between the expectations and the reality, so the correct answer(s) will indicate the prospect of a pliable victim and the result of someone who requires more encouragement from the blackmailer.

Thus, the correct answers are choice D (tractable) and choice F (amenable). The word *sycophantic* indicates a fawning submissiveness that is not entirely implied in the relationship between a blackmailer and the victim. It makes a remote option and not a very good one. The word *patronizing*, with its implication of demeaning behavior, suggests more of the blackmailer's role than the victim's. The word *indolent* indicates laziness, and while a lazy person often needs motivation it is difficult to apply this to the context of the sentence–with the blackmailer's victim being more stubborn against the demands than purely lazy in responding to them. The word *sardonic* makes no sense in the context of the sentence.

23. B, E: The correct answer choices will reflect the contrast between the beginning of the school year and the end of the school year, between the behavior of the children at the beginning of the year and the behavior of the children at the end of the year. Since the sentence indicates that the students all received awards for good behavior at the end of the school year, it stands to reason that their behavior was significantly worse when the school year began. Additionally, the teacher is described as being industrious, or hard-working and productive, so this indicates effort and results on her part.

Thus, the correct answers are choice B (obstreperous) and choice E (unruly). These words indicate a very challenging group of children that required the industrious teacher to roll up her sleeves and work hard. The word *flagrant* might describe the unruly nature of the children–in that they were flagrant in their poor behavior–but it does not make a good description for their actual behavior, as called for in the sentence. The word *boorish* suggests behavior that is rude or impolite, but this is not quite strong enough to offer a solid option. (It also fails to describe third grade children effectively; at the age of 8/9, children are more likely to be described as obstreperous or unruly–that is, out of control due to bad training–than boorish, which has a larger indication of being uncouth simply for the sake of it.) The words *officious* and *sagacious* make no sense in the sentence.

24. C, E: The sentence states that sugar weakens the immune system, particularly during illness, and that it contributes to negative results. As a result, the best answer choices will encompass the suggestion of increasing to the point of making something worse.

Thus, the correct answers are choice C (compound) and choice E (exacerbate). The word *substantiate* does suggest the idea of giving support to something and could be interpreted to mean adding sugar supports the ongoing illness. But this is a round-about way of reading the sentence, and the word *substantiate* does not offer a very good option. The words *belie, ratify,* and *opine* offer nothing except confusion to the meaning of the sentence.

25. B, F: The meaning within the sentence is that despite the clergyman's popularity, the leadership feels the need to remove him from his job and place him in a different role. The correct answer choices will suggest this removal, this stripping of a position with the implication of force. The array of words starting with the letter "d" provides a range of possibilities, and several of them with potential, but only two offer the clear sense of removing or stripping away.

Thus, the correct answers are choice B (divest) and choice F (dispossess). The word *deliberate* only applies to the activities of those persons in leadership, as they decide what to do. The words *decimate* and *demolish* suggest destruction, which may describe the clergyman's feelings, but these words do not express the clear activity of removing him from the job. The word *disconnect* does suggest removal or a broken connection between two items; nonetheless, this word does not suggest the further indication of stripping away. The correct answers will have a somewhat negative connotation: to divest or dispossess is to remove with the element of force or with negative results. To disconnect is simply to detach. Cable can be disconnected. A computer can be disconnected. But these meanings lack the intensity suggested in the sentence and fail to indicate the same element of forced removal that the words *divest* and *dispossess* offer.

Section 5

Quantitative Reasoning

1. B: To determine the value of x, write 10 000 000 000 in scientific notation. Because the number has 10 zeros, it can be written as 10^{10}. Therefore, $10^{10} = 10\,000\,000\,000$ and x = 10. Since 12 is greater than 10, quantity B is greater.

2. A: Write the equation for Line A in slope-intercept form: y = mx + b where m is the slope and b is the y-intercept.

$$10y + 20x = 50$$
$$10y = -20x + 50$$
$$y = -2x + 5$$

Therefore, the slope of Line A is -2 and the y-intercept of Line A is 5. Hence quantity A is greater.

3. C: The ratio of the sides of both triangles is 3:4:5. Therefore, $x = 4$ and $y = 12$. Since $\frac{y}{x} = 3$, both quantities are equal.

4. A: Calculate the income tax Jane paid each month by multiplying the percentage paid in taxes by the monthly income earned.

Month	Income earned ($)	Percentage paid in taxes (%)	Income tax
January	10,000	10	1,000
February	50,000	30	15,000
March	20,000	20	4,000
April	10,000	10	1,000
May	30,000	20	6,000
June	90,000	40	36,000

Jane's average income tax is $\frac{1{,}000+15{,}000+4{,}000+1{,}000+6{,}000+36{,}000}{6} = \$10{,}500$.

Jane's average income is $\frac{10{,}000+50{,}000+20{,}000+10{,}000+30{,}000+90{,}000}{6} = \$35{,}000$, and 22% of $35,000 = $7,700. Therefore, quantity A is greater.

5. A: A prime number is a positive integer that is divisible by exactly two numbers: 1 and itself. A composite number is a positive integer that is divisible by more than just 1 and itself. The number 1 is neither prime nor composite. The smallest composite number greater than 2 is 4, and the smallest prime number less than 10 is 2. Therefore,

$$p = 2, q = 4, and \ \frac{p}{q} = \frac{1}{2} = 0.5$$

6. D: This problem can be solved by the process of elimination. If n is 1, then $\frac{1}{25}$ is less than 1. Similarly, if $n = \sqrt{2}$ or if $n = \frac{1}{2}$, then $\frac{1}{25^{\sqrt{2}}}$ and $\frac{1}{25^{\frac{1}{2}}}$ are both less than 1. However, if $n = -\frac{1}{2}$, then

$$\frac{1}{25^{-\frac{1}{2}}} = 25^{\frac{1}{2}} = \sqrt{25} = 5, \text{ which is greater than 1.}$$

7. B: Angles a and d are alternate interior angles of parallel lines and are therefore congruent. Since angle d measures 45°, angle a measures 45° as well.

8. A: Since RS forms a right angle with line m and angle d measures 45°, angle c measures 45° as well. The measure of angle a is also 45°, making triangle PRS a 45°-45°-90° triangle. Hence, both sides of the triangle are equal. Line RS measures $\frac{\sqrt{2}}{2}$ units longTherefore, line PR is also $\frac{\sqrt{2}}{2}$ units long.

9. A: Triangle PRS is a 45°-45°-90° triangle with sides equal to $\frac{\sqrt{2}}{2}$. Therefore, the hypotenuse of triangle PRS is 1. The hypotenuse of triangle PRS is also the diameter of circle O. Hence, the diameter of circle O is 1.

10. C, D: Write each equation in slope-intercept form: $y = mx + b$, where m is the slope.

$$4y - 12x - 16 = 0$$
$$4y = 12x + 16$$
$$y = 3x + 4$$

and

$$3y - 9x + 18 = 0$$
$$3y = 9x - 18$$
$$y = 3x - 6$$

Both of the equations for choices C and D have slopes of 3. Parallel lines have the same slope.

11. C, D: First, solve the system of equations for x and y. Begin by solving the first equation for x^2.

$$\sqrt{x^2 + y^2} = 5$$
$$x^2 + y^2 = 25$$
$$x^2 = 25 - y^2$$

Next, substitute the equation for x^2 into the second equation.

$$x^2 - y^2 = -7$$
$$25 - y^2 - y^2 = -7$$
$$-2y^2 = -32$$
$$y^2 = 16$$
$$y = 4, -4$$

Substitute either value for y into the second equation:

$$x^2 - y^2 = -7$$
$$x^2 - 16 = -7$$
$$x^2 = 9$$
$$x = 3, -3$$

Since there are two possible values each for *x* and *y*, $x^3 + y^3$ has four possible values:

$$(3)^3 + (4)^3 = 27 + 64 = 91$$
$$(-3)^3 + (4)^3 = -27 + 64 = 37$$
$$(3)^3 + (-4)^3 = 27 - 64 = -37$$
$$(-3)^3 + (-4)^3 = -27 - 64 = -91$$

The first two values are choices C and D.

12. B, D: Based on the coordinate pairs, the length of each side of the square is *P*. The perimeter of the square is the sum of the lengths of the sides. The sum of four sides of length *P* is *P* + *P* + *P* + *P* = 4*P*. If *P* happens to equal 4, then all 4 answers are correct, but only B and D are necessarily correct.

13. B: $A \cup B$ is the union of A and B. The union of two sets is all elements that are in either A or B or both. Therefore, $A \cup B$ is the set of all liberal arts and life science students.

14. A: $A \cap B$ is the intersection of A and B. The intersection of two sets is the set of all elements that are in both A and B. Therefore, $A \cap B$ represents the subset of liberal arts and life science double-majors. According to the diagram, this intersection also represents students who have part-time jobs, but this is not included among the answer choices

15. A, C: Set C is disjoint because it has no elements in common with sets A or B. Therefore, no engineering students also major in liberal arts or life science or both. Also, no engineering students have part-time jobs.

16. $240,000. The value of the house was $300,000, and John and Jane put 20% down. So the down payment was (0.2)($300,000) = $60,000. Therefore, the original loan amount was $300,000 − $60,000 = $240,000.

17. $571,429. The original loan amount of $240,000 represents the principle of the loan According to the graph, the principle was 42% of the total amount they paid throughout the life of the loan. Therefore, the total they paid is $\frac{\$240,000}{0.42} = \$571,429$.

18. 92.9%. The total amount they paid was $571,429. They paid 39% of this total in interest. So, the amount of money they paid in interest was (0.39)($571,429) = $222,857. The original loan amount was $240,000. The percentage of the original loan amount they paid in interest was $\frac{\$222,857}{\$240,000} \cdot 100\% = 92.9\%$.

19. 3.1%. The total interest they paid over 30 years was 92.9% of the original loan amount. Therefore, their average annual interest rate was $\frac{92.9}{30} = 3.1\%$.

20. $108,572. According to the graph, John and Jane paid 19% of the total amount in taxes. The total amount was $571,429.

$$(0.19)(\$571,429) = \$108,572$$

Section 6

Quantitative Reasoning

1. B: First calculate $2\Psi5$.

$$2\Psi\,5 = [(2)(5)]^2 + (2+5)^2$$
$$2\Psi\,5 = 10^2 + 7^2$$
$$2\Psi\,5 = 100 + 49$$
$$2\Psi\,5 = 149$$

Since 149 is less than 150, quantity B is greater.

2. B: Let x represent the number of female students and let y represent the number of students who are US citizens. Because the department has 36 students and twice as many male as female students

$$x + 2x = 36$$
$$3x = 36$$
$$x = 12.$$

Hence, the department has 12 female students. Because the department has three times as many international students as US citizens

$$y + 3y = 36$$
$$4y = 36$$
$$y = 9.$$

The department has 9 students who are US citizens. Hence, quantity B is greater.

3. A: The circumference of a circle is $C = 2\pi r$, where r is the radius of the circle. Since R is the center of the circle, the radius of the circle is r = 2, and the circumference is C = (2)(π)(2) = 4π. Hence, half the circumference is 2π. The area of a triangle is $0.5bh$, where b and h are the base and height of the triangle, respectively. Segment SR represents the base of the triangle and segment QR represents the height. Both the base and height are radii of the circle. So, $b = h = 2$. Therefore, the area of the triangle, $A = (0.5)(2)(2) = 2$. Since 2π is greater than 2, quantity A is greater.

4. B: One can roughly estimate the 2008 GDP of Canada, Japan, and China to be $2, $5, and $5 trillion, which totals $12 trillion. The 2008 GDP of the US is greater than $14 trillion. Therefore, quantity B is greater.

5. C: The class has 100 students, and 60% of the students are male; therefore, the class has 60 male students and 40 female students. 30% of the class, i.e. 30 students, will attend graduate school in computer science. Of the students who will attend graduate school in computer science, the ratio of males to females is 2:1. So, 20 males and 10 females will attend graduate school in computer science. Therefore, 10 of the 40 female students will attend graduate school in computer science. This is 25% of the female students.

6. B: Write the equation for Line Q in slope-intercept form: $y = mx + b$, where m is the slope of the line.

$$5y - 100x - 75 = 0$$
$$5y = 100x + 75$$
$$y = 20x + 15$$

Therefore, the slope of Line Q is 20, and twice the slope is 40. Line B is the only line which has a slope of 40. The slope of Line A and Line C is 20. The slope of Line D is 10.

7. C: According to the table, the list that could represent their hourly wages must have a median of $50.67 and a mean of $57.44. The median is the middle value in a set of numbers arranged in increasing order. Because the set of numbers in this problem has four values, the median is the average of the middle two values. The average of the middle two values for choice C is $50.67. The mean is the average of a set of numbers, and the average wage in choice C is $57.44. Visual inspection of the wages in choice A reveal the mean is not $57.44. Visual inspection of wages in choice B show the median is not $50.67. Both the median and mean are incorrect for the wages in choice D.

8. D: The inequality which represents the given scenario is $87,980 + 87980x > 119,480$, where x is the decimal representation of the percent increase in annual salary. Solve the inequality for x:

$$87,980 + 87980x > 119,480$$
$$87,980(1 + x) > 119,480$$
$$1 + x > 1.358036$$
$$x > 0.358036$$

Therefore, the mean annual salary for those working in the fields of computers and mathematics must be raised by more than 35.8% to exceed the mean annual salary earned by those in management.

9. B: Set up and solve an equation to determine how many hours a week the cook must work to earn an annual salary of $58,000: $(\$10.57)(x)(52) = \$58,000$, where x represents the number of hours the cook must work each of the 52 weeks of the year. Since x is approximately equal to 106 and since a 40-hour work week is standard, the cook must work $106 - 40 = 66$ additional hours each week in order to earn the same annual wage as a librarian.

10. B: As a junior associate, the lawyer currently earns an annual salary of $119,120 plus overtime pay equivalent to 25% of her 40 hour salary (10/40 = 25%). Therefore, her total annual compensation for working 50 hours per week is (1.25)($119,120) = $148,900. As a senior associate with a 25% raise, she would earn the same annual salary ($148,900) but would be working 15 hours of overtime every week instead of 10. Therefore, this promotion is not in her best financial interest.

11. A, D:

$$(A^2)(A^9) = A^{2+9} = A^{11}.$$

$$\frac{A^9}{A^2} = A^{9-2} = A^7.$$

12. A, B: Side z is the hypotenuse of a right triangle, and the hypotenuse is the longest side. Therefore, the other two sides can hold any value less than the hypotenuse as long as the Pythagorean Theorem is satisfied.

13. B: Since $\frac{b}{a} = 2, b = 60°$ and $a = 30°$. Therefore, this is a 30°-60°-90° triangle. Since $x = 1, y = \sqrt{3}$ and $z = 2$.

14. A, B: If the ages of all three siblings are contained within the choices given, then the siblings' ages are either (2, 4, 8) or (4, 8, 16). Since Jill is the youngest of the three, she could only be 2 or 4.

15. B, C: The distance between points (0,0) and (0,3) is 3 units along the y-axis. The distance between points (0,0) and (4,0) is 4 units along the x-axis. The triangle described is a right triangle with a hypotenuse 5 units long.

16. 180. The area of a single square is $A = s^2$ where s is the length of one side of the square. In this case, the length of one side of a single square is 6. Therefore, the area of a single square is $6^2 = 36$. The sum of the areas of the five squares is $5A = (5)(36) = 180$.

17. 8.5. Side BC is the hypotenuse of a right triangle, it can be found by using the Pythagorean Theorem: $a^2 + b^2 = c^2$, where a and b are sides of the triangle and c is the hypotenuse. The length of both sides of the triangle is 6. Hence,

$$6^2 + 6^2 = c^2$$
$$36 + 36 = c^2$$
$$\sqrt{36 + 36} = c$$
$$\sqrt{72} = c$$
$$8.5 = c$$

18. 18. The area of a triangle is $A = \frac{1}{2}bh$ where b and h are the lengths of the triangle's base and height, respectively. In this case, both b and h are sides of square S. Therefore,

$b = h = 6$, and the area of the triangle is $\frac{1}{2}(6)(6) = 18$.

19. 58.0. The perimeter of the octagon is the sum of the lengths of its sides. The lengths of sides $AB = CD = EF = GH = 6$, and the lengths of sides $BC = DE = FG = AH = 8.5$. (See explanation for question 17.) Therefore, the sum of the lengths is $(4)(6) + (4)(8.5) = 24 + 34 = 58$.

20. 252. The area of the octagon is the sum of the areas of the five squares and four triangles. The area of a single square is 36. (See the explanation for question 16.) The area of a single triangle is 18. (See the explanation for question 18.) Therefore, the area of the octagon is $A = (5)(36) + (4)(18) = 180 + 72 = 252$.

How to Overcome Test Anxiety

Just the thought of taking a test is enough to make most people a little nervous. A test is an important event that can have a long-term impact on your future, so it's important to take it seriously and it's natural to feel anxious about performing well. But just because anxiety is normal, that doesn't mean that it's helpful in test taking, or that you should simply accept it as part of your life. Anxiety can have a variety of effects. These effects can be mild, like making you feel slightly nervous, or severe, like blocking your ability to focus or remember even a simple detail.

If you experience test anxiety—whether severe or mild—it's important to know how to beat it. To discover this, first you need to understand what causes test anxiety.

Causes of Test Anxiety

While we often think of anxiety as an uncontrollable emotional state, it can actually be caused by simple, practical things. One of the most common causes of test anxiety is that a person does not feel adequately prepared for their test. This feeling can be the result of many different issues such as poor study habits or lack of organization, but the most common culprit is time management. Starting to study too late, failing to organize your study time to cover all of the material, or being distracted while you study will mean that you're not well prepared for the test. This may lead to cramming the night before, which will cause you to be physically and mentally exhausted for the test. Poor time management also contributes to feelings of stress, fear, and hopelessness as you realize you are not well prepared but don't know what to do about it.

Other times, test anxiety is not related to your preparation for the test but comes from unresolved fear. This may be a past failure on a test, or poor performance on tests in general. It may come from comparing yourself to others who seem to be performing better or from the stress of living up to expectations. Anxiety may be driven by fears of the future—how failure on this test would affect your educational and career goals. These fears are often completely irrational, but they can still negatively impact your test performance.

Review Video: <u>3 Reasons You Have Test Anxiety</u>
Visit mometrix.com/academy and enter code: 428468

Elements of Test Anxiety

As mentioned earlier, test anxiety is considered to be an emotional state, but it has physical and mental components as well. Sometimes you may not even realize that you are suffering from test anxiety until you notice the physical symptoms. These can include trembling hands, rapid heartbeat, sweating, nausea, and tense muscles. Extreme anxiety may lead to fainting or vomiting. Obviously, any of these symptoms can have a negative impact on testing. It is important to recognize them as soon as they begin to occur so that you can address the problem before it damages your performance.

Review Video: 3 Ways to Tell You Have Test Anxiety
Visit mometrix.com/academy and enter code: 927847

The mental components of test anxiety include trouble focusing and inability to remember learned information. During a test, your mind is on high alert, which can help you recall information and stay focused for an extended period of time. However, anxiety interferes with your mind's natural processes, causing you to blank out, even on the questions you know well. The strain of testing during anxiety makes it difficult to stay focused, especially on a test that may take several hours. Extreme anxiety can take a huge mental toll, making it difficult not only to recall test information but even to understand the test questions or pull your thoughts together.

Review Video: How Test Anxiety Affects Memory
Visit mometrix.com/academy and enter code: 609003

Effects of Test Anxiety

Test anxiety is like a disease—if left untreated, it will get progressively worse. Anxiety leads to poor performance, and this reinforces the feelings of fear and failure, which in turn lead to poor performances on subsequent tests. It can grow from a mild nervousness to a crippling condition. If allowed to progress, test anxiety can have a big impact on your schooling, and consequently on your future.

Test anxiety can spread to other parts of your life. Anxiety on tests can become anxiety in any stressful situation, and blanking on a test can turn into panicking in a job situation. But fortunately, you don't have to let anxiety rule your testing and determine your grades. There are a number of relatively simple steps you can take to move past anxiety and function normally on a test and in the rest of life.

Review Video: How Test Anxiety Impacts Your Grades
Visit mometrix.com/academy and enter code: 939819

Physical Steps for Beating Test Anxiety

While test anxiety is a serious problem, the good news is that it can be overcome. It doesn't have to control your ability to think and remember information. While it may take time, you can begin taking steps today to beat anxiety.

Just as your first hint that you may be struggling with anxiety comes from the physical symptoms, the first step to treating it is also physical. Rest is crucial for having a clear, strong mind. If you are tired, it is much easier to give in to anxiety. But if you establish good sleep habits, your body and mind will be ready to perform optimally, without the strain of exhaustion. Additionally, sleeping well helps you to retain information better, so you're more likely to recall the answers when you see the test questions.

Getting good sleep means more than going to bed on time. It's important to allow your brain time to relax. Take study breaks from time to time so it doesn't get overworked, and don't study right before bed. Take time to rest your mind before trying to rest your body, or you may find it difficult to fall asleep.

Review Video: The Importance of Sleep for Your Brain
Visit mometrix.com/academy and enter code: 319338

Along with sleep, other aspects of physical health are important in preparing for a test. Good nutrition is vital for good brain function. Sugary foods and drinks may give a burst of energy but this burst is followed by a crash, both physically and emotionally. Instead, fuel your body with protein and vitamin-rich foods.

Also, drink plenty of water. Dehydration can lead to headaches and exhaustion, especially if your brain is already under stress from the rigors of the test. Particularly if your test is a long one, drink water during the breaks. And if possible, take an energy-boosting snack to eat between sections.

Review Video: How Diet Can Affect your Mood
Visit mometrix.com/academy and enter code: 624317

Along with sleep and diet, a third important part of physical health is exercise. Maintaining a steady workout schedule is helpful, but even taking 5-minute study breaks to walk can help get your blood pumping faster and clear your head. Exercise also releases endorphins, which contribute to a positive feeling and can help combat test anxiety.

When you nurture your physical health, you are also contributing to your mental health. If your body is healthy, your mind is much more likely to be healthy as well. So take time to rest, nourish your body with healthy food and water, and get moving as much as possible. Taking these physical steps will make you stronger and more able to take the mental steps necessary to overcome test anxiety.

Review Video: How to Stay Healthy and Prevent Test Anxiety
Visit mometrix.com/academy and enter code: 877894

Mental Steps for Beating Test Anxiety

Working on the mental side of test anxiety can be more challenging, but as with the physical side, there are clear steps you can take to overcome it. As mentioned earlier, test anxiety often stems from lack of preparation, so the obvious solution is to prepare for the test. Effective studying may be the most important weapon you have for beating test anxiety, but you can and should employ several other mental tools to combat fear.

First, boost your confidence by reminding yourself of past success—tests or projects that you aced. If you're putting as much effort into preparing for this test as you did for those, there's no reason you should expect to fail here. Work hard to prepare; then trust your preparation.

Second, surround yourself with encouraging people. It can be helpful to find a study group, but be sure that the people you're around will encourage a positive attitude. If you spend time with others who are anxious or cynical, this will only contribute to your own anxiety. Look for others who are motivated to study hard from a desire to succeed, not from a fear of failure.

Third, reward yourself. A test is physically and mentally tiring, even without anxiety, and it can be helpful to have something to look forward to. Plan an activity following the test, regardless of the outcome, such as going to a movie or getting ice cream.

When you are taking the test, if you find yourself beginning to feel anxious, remind yourself that you know the material. Visualize successfully completing the test. Then take a few deep, relaxing breaths and return to it. Work through the questions carefully but with confidence, knowing that you are capable of succeeding.

Developing a healthy mental approach to test taking will also aid in other areas of life. Test anxiety affects more than just the actual test—it can be damaging to your mental health and even contribute to depression. It's important to beat test anxiety before it becomes a problem for more than testing.

Review Video: <u>Test Anxiety and Depression</u>
Visit mometrix.com/academy and enter code: 904704

Study Strategy

Being prepared for the test is necessary to combat anxiety, but what does being prepared look like? You may study for hours on end and still not feel prepared. What you need is a strategy for test prep. The next few pages outline our recommended steps to help you plan out and conquer the challenge of preparation.

STEP 1: SCOPE OUT THE TEST

Learn everything you can about the format (multiple choice, essay, etc.) and what will be on the test. Gather any study materials, course outlines, or sample exams that may be available. Not only will this help you to prepare, but knowing what to expect can help to alleviate test anxiety.

STEP 2: MAP OUT THE MATERIAL

Look through the textbook or study guide and make note of how many chapters or sections it has. Then divide these over the time you have. For example, if a book has 15 chapters and you have five days to study, you need to cover three chapters each day. Even better, if you have the time, leave an extra day at the end for overall review after you have gone through the material in depth.

If time is limited, you may need to prioritize the material. Look through it and make note of which sections you think you already have a good grasp on, and which need review. While you are studying, skim quickly through the familiar sections and take more time on the challenging parts. Write out your plan so you don't get lost as you go. Having a written plan also helps you feel more in control of the study, so anxiety is less likely to arise from feeling overwhelmed at the amount to cover.

STEP 3: GATHER YOUR TOOLS

Decide what study method works best for you. Do you prefer to highlight in the book as you study and then go back over the highlighted portions? Or do you type out notes of the important information? Or is it helpful to make flashcards that you can carry with you? Assemble the pens, index cards, highlighters, post-it notes, and any other materials you may need so you won't be distracted by getting up to find things while you study.

If you're having a hard time retaining the information or organizing your notes, experiment with different methods. For example, try color-coding by subject with colored pens, highlighters, or post-it notes. If you learn better by hearing, try recording yourself reading your notes so you can listen while in the car, working out, or simply sitting at your desk. Ask a friend to quiz you from your flashcards, or try teaching someone the material to solidify it in your mind.

STEP 4: CREATE YOUR ENVIRONMENT

It's important to avoid distractions while you study. This includes both the obvious distractions like visitors and the subtle distractions like an uncomfortable chair (or a too-comfortable couch that makes you want to fall asleep). Set up the best study environment possible: good lighting and a comfortable work area. If background music helps you focus, you may want to turn it on, but otherwise keep the room quiet. If you are using a computer to take notes, be sure you don't have any other windows open, especially applications like social media, games, or anything else that could distract you. Silence your phone and turn off notifications. Be sure to keep water close by so you stay hydrated while you study (but avoid unhealthy drinks and snacks).

Also, take into account the best time of day to study. Are you freshest first thing in the morning? Try to set aside some time then to work through the material. Is your mind clearer in the afternoon or evening? Schedule your study session then. Another method is to study at the same time of day that you will take the test, so that your brain gets used to working on the material at that time and will be ready to focus at test time.

STEP 5: STUDY!

Once you have done all the study preparation, it's time to settle into the actual studying. Sit down, take a few moments to settle your mind so you can focus, and begin to follow your study plan. Don't give in to distractions or let yourself procrastinate. This is your time to prepare so you'll be ready to fearlessly approach the test. Make the most of the time and stay focused.

Of course, you don't want to burn out. If you study too long you may find that you're not retaining the information very well. Take regular study breaks. For example, taking five minutes out of every hour to walk briskly, breathing deeply and swinging your arms, can help your mind stay fresh.

As you get to the end of each chapter or section, it's a good idea to do a quick review. Remind yourself of what you learned and work on any difficult parts. When you feel that you've mastered the material, move on to the next part. At the end of your study session, briefly skim through your notes again.

But while review is helpful, cramming last minute is NOT. If at all possible, work ahead so that you won't need to fit all your study into the last day. Cramming overloads your brain with more information than it can process and retain, and your tired mind may struggle to recall even previously learned information when it is overwhelmed with last-minute study. Also, the urgent nature of cramming and the stress placed on your brain contribute to anxiety. You'll be more likely to go to the test feeling unprepared and having trouble thinking clearly.

So don't cram, and don't stay up late before the test, even just to review your notes at a leisurely pace. Your brain needs rest more than it needs to go over the information again. In fact, plan to finish your studies by noon or early afternoon the day before the test. Give your brain the rest of the day to relax or focus on other things, and get a good night's sleep. Then you will be fresh for the test and better able to recall what you've studied.

STEP 6: TAKE A PRACTICE TEST

Many courses offer sample tests, either online or in the study materials. This is an excellent resource to check whether you have mastered the material, as well as to prepare for the test format and environment.

Check the test format ahead of time: the number of questions, the type (multiple choice, free response, etc.), and the time limit. Then create a plan for working through them. For example, if you have 30 minutes to take a 60-question test, your limit is 30 seconds per question. Spend less time on the questions you know well so that you can take more time on the difficult ones.

If you have time to take several practice tests, take the first one open book, with no time limit. Work through the questions at your own pace and make sure you fully understand them. Gradually work up to taking a test under test conditions: sit at a desk with all study materials put away and set a timer. Pace yourself to make sure you finish the test with time to spare and go back to check your answers if you have time.

After each test, check your answers. On the questions you missed, be sure you understand why you missed them. Did you misread the question (tests can use tricky wording)? Did you forget the information? Or was it something you hadn't learned? Go back and study any shaky areas that the practice tests reveal.

Taking these tests not only helps with your grade, but also aids in combating test anxiety. If you're already used to the test conditions, you're less likely to worry about it, and working through tests until you're scoring well gives you a confidence boost. Go through the practice tests until you feel comfortable, and then you can go into the test knowing that you're ready for it.

Test Tips

On test day, you should be confident, knowing that you've prepared well and are ready to answer the questions. But aside from preparation, there are several test day strategies you can employ to maximize your performance.

First, as stated before, get a good night's sleep the night before the test (and for several nights before that, if possible). Go into the test with a fresh, alert mind rather than staying up late to study.

Try not to change too much about your normal routine on the day of the test. It's important to eat a nutritious breakfast, but if you normally don't eat breakfast at all, consider eating just a protein bar. If you're a coffee drinker, go ahead and have your normal coffee. Just make sure you time it so that the caffeine doesn't wear off right in the middle of your test. Avoid sugary beverages, and drink enough water to stay hydrated but not so much that you need a restroom break 10 minutes into the test. If your test isn't first thing in the morning, consider going for a walk or doing a light workout before the test to get your blood flowing.

Allow yourself enough time to get ready, and leave for the test with plenty of time to spare so you won't have the anxiety of scrambling to arrive in time. Another reason to be early is to select a good seat. It's helpful to sit away from doors and windows, which can be distracting. Find a good seat, get out your supplies, and settle your mind before the test begins.

When the test begins, start by going over the instructions carefully, even if you already know what to expect. Make sure you avoid any careless mistakes by following the directions.

Then begin working through the questions, pacing yourself as you've practiced. If you're not sure on an answer, don't spend too much time on it, and don't let it shake your confidence. Either skip it and come back later, or eliminate as many wrong answers as possible and guess among the remaining ones. Don't dwell on these questions as you continue—put them out of your mind and focus on what lies ahead.

Be sure to read all of the answer choices, even if you're sure the first one is the right answer. Sometimes you'll find a better one if you keep reading. But don't second-guess yourself if you do immediately know the answer. Your gut instinct is usually right. Don't let test anxiety rob you of the information you know.

If you have time at the end of the test (and if the test format allows), go back and review your answers. Be cautious about changing any, since your first instinct tends to be correct, but make sure you didn't misread any of the questions or accidentally mark the wrong answer choice. Look over any you skipped and make an educated guess.

At the end, leave the test feeling confident. You've done your best, so don't waste time worrying about your performance or wishing you could change anything. Instead, celebrate the successful completion of this test. And finally, use this test to learn how to deal with anxiety even better next time.

Important Qualification

Not all anxiety is created equal. If your test anxiety is causing major issues in your life beyond the classroom or testing center, or if you are experiencing troubling physical symptoms related to your anxiety, it may be a sign of a serious physiological or psychological condition. If this sounds like your situation, we strongly encourage you to seek professional help.

How to Overcome Your Fear of Math

The word *math* is enough to strike fear into most hearts. How many of us have memories of sitting through confusing lectures, wrestling over mind-numbing homework, or taking tests that still seem incomprehensible even after hours of study? Years after graduation, many still shudder at these memories.

The fact is, math is not just a classroom subject. It has real-world implications that you face every day, whether you realize it or not. This may be balancing your monthly budget, deciding how many supplies to buy for a project, or simply splitting a meal check with friends. The idea of daily confrontations with math can be so paralyzing that some develop a condition known as *math anxiety*.

But you do NOT need to be paralyzed by this anxiety! In fact, while you may have thought all your life that you're not good at math, or that your brain isn't wired to understand it, the truth is that you may have been conditioned to think this way. From your earliest school days, the way you were taught affected the way you viewed different subjects. And the way math has been taught has changed.

Several decades ago, there was a shift in American math classrooms. The focus changed from traditional problem-solving to a conceptual view of topics, de-emphasizing the importance of learning the basics and building on them. The solid foundation necessary for math progression and confidence was undermined. Math became more of a vague concept than a concrete idea. Today, it is common to think of math, not as a straightforward system, but as a mysterious, complicated method that can't be fully understood unless you're a genius.

This is why you may still have nightmares about being called on to answer a difficult problem in front of the class. Math anxiety is a very real, though unnecessary, fear.

Math anxiety may begin with a single class period. Let's say you missed a day in 6th grade math and never quite understood the concept that was taught while you were gone. Since math is cumulative, with each new concept building on past ones, this could very well affect the rest of your math career. Without that one day's knowledge, it will be difficult to understand any other concepts that link to it. Rather than realizing that you're just missing one key piece, you may begin to believe that you're simply not capable of understanding math.

This belief can change the way you approach other classes, career options, and everyday life experiences, if you become anxious at the thought that math might be required. A student who loves science may choose a different path of study upon realizing that multiple math classes will be required for a degree. An aspiring medical student may hesitate at the thought of going through the necessary math classes. For some this anxiety escalates into a more extreme state known as *math phobia*.

Math anxiety is challenging to address because it is rooted deeply and may come from a variety of causes: an embarrassing moment in class, a teacher who did not explain concepts well and contributed to a shaky foundation, or a failed test that contributed to the belief of math failure.

These causes add up over time, encouraged by society's popular view that math is hard and unpleasant. Eventually a person comes to firmly believe that he or she is simply bad at math. This belief makes it difficult to grasp new concepts or even remember old ones. Homework and test

128

grades begin to slip, which only confirms the belief. The poor performance is not due to lack of ability but is caused by math anxiety.

Math anxiety is an emotional issue, not a lack of intelligence. But when it becomes deeply rooted, it can become more than just an emotional problem. Physical symptoms appear. Blood pressure may rise and heartbeat may quicken at the sight of a math problem – or even the thought of math! This fear leads to a mental block. When someone with math anxiety is asked to perform a calculation, even a basic problem can seem overwhelming and impossible. The emotional and physical response to the thought of math prevents the brain from working through it logically.

The more this happens, the more a person's confidence drops, and the more math anxiety is generated. This vicious cycle must be broken!

The first step in breaking the cycle is to go back to very beginning and make sure you really understand the basics of how math works and why it works. It is not enough to memorize rules for multiplication and division. If you don't know WHY these rules work, your foundation will be shaky and you will be at risk of developing a phobia. Understanding mathematical concepts not only promotes confidence and security, but allows you to build on this understanding for new concepts. Additionally, you can solve unfamiliar problems using familiar concepts and processes.

Why is it that students in other countries regularly outperform American students in math? The answer likely boils down to a couple of things: the foundation of mathematical conceptual understanding and societal perception. While students in the US are not expected to *like* or *get* math, in many other nations, students are expected not only to understand math but also to excel at it.

Changing the American view of math that leads to math anxiety is a monumental task. It requires changing the training of teachers nationwide, from kindergarten through high school, so that they learn to teach the *why* behind math and to combat the wrong math views that students may develop. It also involves changing the stigma associated with math, so that it is no longer viewed as unpleasant and incomprehensible. While these are necessary changes, they are challenging and will take time. But in the meantime, math anxiety is not irreversible—it can be faced and defeated, one person at a time.

False Beliefs

One reason math anxiety has taken such hold is that several false beliefs have been created and shared until they became widely accepted. Some of these unhelpful beliefs include the following:

There is only one way to solve a math problem. In the same way that you can choose from different driving routes and still arrive at the same house, you can solve a math problem using different methods and still find the correct answer. A person who understands the reasoning behind math calculations may be able to look at an unfamiliar concept and find the right answer, just by applying logic to the knowledge they already have. This approach may be different than what is taught in the classroom, but it is still valid. Unfortunately, even many teachers view math as a subject where the best course of action is to memorize the rule or process for each problem rather than as a place for students to exercise logic and creativity in finding a solution.

Many people don't have a mind for math. A person who has struggled due to poor teaching or math anxiety may falsely believe that he or she doesn't have the mental capacity to grasp mathematical concepts. Most of the time, this is false. Many people find that when they are relieved of their math anxiety, they have more than enough brainpower to understand math.

Men are naturally better at math than women. Even though research has shown this to be false, many young women still avoid math careers and classes because of their belief that their math abilities are inferior. Many girls have come to believe that math is a male skill and have given up trying to understand or enjoy it.

Counting aids are bad. Something like counting on your fingers or drawing out a problem to visualize it may be frowned on as childish or a crutch, but these devices can help you get a tangible understanding of a problem or a concept.

Sadly, many students buy into these ideologies at an early age. A young girl who enjoys math class may be conditioned to think that she doesn't actually have the brain for it because math is for boys, and may turn her energies to other pursuits, permanently closing the door on a wide range of opportunities. A child who finds the right answer but doesn't follow the teacher's method may believe that he is doing it wrong and isn't good at math. A student who never had a problem with math before may have a poor teacher and become confused, yet believe that the problem is because she doesn't have a mathematical mind.

Students who have bought into these erroneous beliefs quickly begin to add their own anxieties, adapting them to their own personal situations:

I'll never use this in real life. A huge number of people wrongly believe that math is irrelevant outside the classroom. By adopting this mindset, they are handicapping themselves for a life in a mathematical world, as well as limiting their career choices. When they are inevitably faced with real-world math, they are conditioning themselves to respond with anxiety.

I'm not quick enough. While timed tests and quizzes, or even simply comparing yourself with other students in the class, can lead to this belief, speed is not an indicator of skill level. A person can work very slowly yet understand at a deep level.

If I can understand it, it's too easy. People with a low view of their own abilities tend to think that if they are able to grasp a concept, it must be simple. They cannot accept the idea that they are capable of understanding math. This belief will make it harder to learn, no matter how intelligent they are.

I just can't learn this. An overwhelming number of people think this, from young children to adults, and much of the time it is simply not true. But this mindset can turn into a self-fulfilling prophecy that keeps you from exercising and growing your math ability.

The good news is, each of these myths can be debunked. For most people, they are based on emotion and psychology, NOT on actual ability! It will take time, effort, and the desire to change, but change is possible. Even if you have spent years thinking that you don't have the capability to understand math, it is not too late to uncover your true ability and find relief from the anxiety that surrounds math.

Math Strategies

It is important to have a plan of attack to combat math anxiety. There are many useful strategies for pinpointing the fears or myths and eradicating them:

Go back to the basics. For most people, math anxiety stems from a poor foundation. You may think that you have a complete understanding of addition and subtraction, or even decimals and percentages, but make absolutely sure. Learning math is different from learning other subjects. For example, when you learn history, you study various time periods and places and events. It may be important to memorize dates or find out about the lives of famous people. When you move from US history to world history, there will be some overlap, but a large amount of the information will be new. Mathematical concepts, on the other hand, are very closely linked and highly dependent on each other. It's like climbing a ladder – if a rung is missing from your understanding, it may be difficult or impossible for you to climb any higher, no matter how hard you try. So go back and make sure your math foundation is strong. This may mean taking a remedial math course, going to a tutor to work through the shaky concepts, or just going through your old homework to make sure you really understand it.

Speak the language. Math has a large vocabulary of terms and phrases unique to working problems. Sometimes these are completely new terms, and sometimes they are common words, but are used differently in a math setting. If you can't speak the language, it will be very difficult to get a thorough understanding of the concepts. It's common for students to think that they don't understand math when they simply don't understand the vocabulary. The good news is that this is fairly easy to fix. Brushing up on any terms you aren't quite sure of can help bring the rest of the concepts into focus.

Check your anxiety level. When you think about math, do you feel nervous or uncomfortable? Do you struggle with feelings of inadequacy, even on concepts that you know you've already learned? It's important to understand your specific math anxieties, and what triggers them. When you catch yourself falling back on a false belief, mentally replace it with the truth. Don't let yourself believe that you can't learn, or that struggling with a concept means you'll never understand it. Instead, remind yourself of how much you've already learned and dwell on that past success. Visualize grasping the new concept, linking it to your old knowledge, and moving on to the next challenge. Also, learn how to manage anxiety when it arises. There are many techniques for coping with the irrational fears that rise to the surface when you enter the math classroom. This may include controlled breathing, replacing negative thoughts with positive ones, or visualizing success. Anxiety interferes with your ability to concentrate and absorb information, which in turn contributes to greater anxiety. If you can learn how to regain control of your thinking, you will be better able to pay attention, make progress, and succeed!

Don't go it alone. Like any deeply ingrained belief, math anxiety is not easy to eradicate. And there is no need for you to wrestle through it on your own. It will take time, and many people find that speaking with a counselor or psychiatrist helps. They can help you develop strategies for responding to anxiety and overcoming old ideas. Additionally, it can be very helpful to take a short course or seek out a math tutor to help you find and fix the missing rungs on your ladder and make sure that you're ready to progress to the next level. You can also find a number of math aids online: courses that will teach you mental devices for figuring out problems, how to get the most out of your math classes, etc.

Check your math attitude. No matter how much you want to learn and overcome your anxiety, you'll have trouble if you still have a negative attitude toward math. If you think it's too hard, or just

131

have general feelings of dread about math, it will be hard to learn and to break through the anxiety. Work on cultivating a positive math attitude. Remind yourself that math is not just a hurdle to be cleared, but a valuable asset. When you view math with a positive attitude, you'll be much more likely to understand and even enjoy it. This is something you must do for yourself. You may find it helpful to visit with a counselor. Your tutor, friends, and family may cheer you on in your endeavors. But your greatest asset is yourself. You are inside your own mind – tell yourself what you need to hear. Relive past victories. Remind yourself that you are capable of understanding math. Root out any false beliefs that linger and replace them with positive truths. Even if it doesn't feel true at first, it will begin to affect your thinking and pave the way for a positive, anxiety-free mindset.

Aside from these general strategies, there are a number of specific practical things you can do to begin your journey toward overcoming math anxiety. Something as simple as learning a new note-taking strategy can change the way you approach math and give you more confidence and understanding. New study techniques can also make a huge difference.

Math anxiety leads to bad habits. If it causes you to be afraid of answering a question in class, you may gravitate toward the back row. You may be embarrassed to ask for help. And you may procrastinate on assignments, which leads to rushing through them at the last moment when it's too late to get a better understanding. It's important to identify your negative behaviors and replace them with positive ones:

Prepare ahead of time. Read the lesson before you go to class. Being exposed to the topics that will be covered in class ahead of time, even if you don't understand them perfectly, is extremely helpful in increasing what you retain from the lecture. Do your homework and, if you're still shaky, go over some extra problems. The key to a solid understanding of math is practice.

Sit front and center. When you can easily see and hear, you'll understand more, and you'll avoid the distractions of other students if no one is in front of you. Plus, you're more likely to be sitting with students who are positive and engaged, rather than others with math anxiety. Let their positive math attitude rub off on you.

Ask questions in class and out. If you don't understand something, just ask. If you need a more in-depth explanation, the teacher may need to work with you outside of class, but often it's a simple concept you don't quite understand, and a single question may clear it up. If you wait, you may not be able to follow the rest of the day's lesson. For extra help, most professors have office hours outside of class when you can go over concepts one-on-one to clear up any uncertainties. Additionally, there may be a *math lab* or study session you can attend for homework help. Take advantage of this.

Review. Even if you feel that you've fully mastered a concept, review it periodically to reinforce it. Going over an old lesson has several benefits: solidifying your understanding, giving you a confidence boost, and even giving some new insights into material that you're currently learning! Don't let yourself get rusty. That can lead to problems with learning later concepts.

Teaching Tips

While the math student's mindset is the most crucial to overcoming math anxiety, it is also important for others to adjust their math attitudes. Teachers and parents have an enormous influence on how students relate to math. They can either contribute to math confidence or math anxiety.

As a parent or teacher, it is very important to convey a positive math attitude. Retelling horror stories of your own bad experience with math will contribute to a new generation of math anxiety. Even if you don't share your experiences, others will be able to sense your fears and may begin to believe them.

Even a careless comment can have a big impact, so watch for phrases like *He's not good at math* or *I never liked math.* You are a crucial role model, and your children or students will unconsciously adopt your mindset. Give them a positive example to follow. Rather than teaching them to fear the math world before they even know it, teach them about all its potential and excitement.

Work to present math as an integral, beautiful, and understandable part of life. Encourage creativity in solving problems. Watch for false beliefs and dispel them. Cross the lines between subjects: integrate history, English, and music with math. Show students how math is used every day, and how the entire world is based on mathematical principles, from the pull of gravity to the shape of seashells. Instead of letting students see math as a necessary evil, direct them to view it as an imaginative, beautiful art form – an art form that they are capable of mastering and using.

Don't give too narrow a view of math. It is more than just numbers. Yes, working problems and learning formulas is a large part of classroom math. But don't let the teaching stop there. Teach students about the everyday implications of math. Show them how nature works according to the laws of mathematics, and take them outside to make discoveries of their own. Expose them to math-related careers by inviting visiting speakers, asking students to do research and presentations, and learning students' interests and aptitudes on a personal level.

Demonstrate the importance of math. Many people see math as nothing more than a required stepping stone to their degree, a nuisance with no real usefulness. Teach students that algebra is used every day in managing their bank accounts, in following recipes, and in scheduling the day's events. Show them how learning to do geometric proofs helps them to develop logical thinking, an invaluable life skill. Let them see that math surrounds them and is integrally linked to their daily lives: that weather predictions are based on math, that math was used to design cars and other machines, etc. Most of all, give them the tools to use math to enrich their lives.

Make math as tangible as possible. Use visual aids and objects that can be touched. It is much easier to grasp a concept when you can hold it in your hands and manipulate it, rather than just listening to the lecture. Encourage math outside of the classroom. The real world is full of measuring, counting, and calculating, so let students participate in this. Keep your eyes open for numbers and patterns to discuss. Talk about how scores are calculated in sports games and how far apart plants are placed in a garden row for maximum growth. Build the mindset that math is a normal and interesting part of daily life.

Finally, find math resources that help to build a positive math attitude. There are a number of books that show math as fascinating and exciting while teaching important concepts, for example: *The Math Curse; A Wrinkle in Time; The Phantom Tollbooth;* and *Fractals, Googols and Other Mathematical Tales.* You can also find a number of online resources: math puzzles and games,

133

videos that show math in nature, and communities of math enthusiasts. On a local level, students can compete in a variety of math competitions with other schools or join a math club.

The student who experiences math as exciting and interesting is unlikely to suffer from math anxiety. Going through life without this handicap is an immense advantage and opens many doors that others have closed through their fear.

Self-Check

Whether you suffer from math anxiety or not, chances are that you have been exposed to some of the false beliefs mentioned above. Now is the time to check yourself for any errors you may have accepted. Do you think you're not wired for math? Or that you don't need to understand it since you're not planning on a math career? Do you think math is just too difficult for the average person?

Find the errors you've taken to heart and replace them with positive thinking. Are you capable of learning math? Yes! Can you control your anxiety? Yes! These errors will resurface from time to time, so be watchful. Don't let others with math anxiety influence you or sway your confidence. If you're having trouble with a concept, find help. Don't let it discourage you!

Create a plan of attack for defeating math anxiety and sharpening your skills. Do some research and decide if it would help you to take a class, get a tutor, or find some online resources to fine-tune your knowledge. Make the effort to get good nutrition, hydration, and sleep so that you are operating at full capacity. Remind yourself daily that you are skilled and that anxiety does not control you. Your mind is capable of so much more than you know. Give it the tools it needs to grow and thrive.

Thank You

We at Mometrix would like to extend our heartfelt thanks to you, our friend and patron, for allowing us to play a part in your journey. It is a privilege to serve people from all walks of life who are unified in their commitment to building the best future they can for themselves.

The preparation you devote to these important testing milestones may be the most valuable educational opportunity you have for making a real difference in your life. We encourage you to put your heart into it—that feeling of succeeding, overcoming, and yes, conquering will be well worth the hours you've invested.

We want to hear your story, your struggles and your successes, and if you see any opportunities for us to improve our materials so we can help others even more effectively in the future, please share that with us as well. **The team at Mometrix would be absolutely thrilled to hear from you!** So please, send us an email (support@mometrix.com) and let's stay in touch.

> **If you'd like some additional help, check out these other resources we offer for your exam:**
> **http://mometrixflashcards.com/GRE**

Additional Bonus Material

Due to our efforts to try to keep this book to a manageable length, we've created a link that will give you access to all of your additional bonus material.

Please visit https://www.mometrix.com/bonus948/gre to access the information.

Made in the USA
Columbia, SC
14 January 2020